Southern Living®

ALL-TIME FAVORITE

DESSERT
RECIPES

Southern Living®

ALL-TIME FAVORITE
DESSERT
RECIPES

Compiled and Edited by
Jean Wickstrom Liles

Oxmoor
House®

Library of Congress Catalog Number: 96-67714
ISBN: 0-8487-2228-0
Manufactured in the United States of America
First Printing 1996

Editor-in-Chief: Nancy Fitzpatrick Wyatt
Editorial Director, Special Interest Publications: Ann H. Harvey
Senior Foods Editor: Susan Carlisle Payne
Senior Editor, Editorial Services: Olivia Kindig Wells
Art Director: James Boone

Southern Living® ALL-TIME FAVORITE DESSERT RECIPES

Menu and Recipe Consultant: Jean Wickstrom Liles
Assistant Editor: Kelly Hooper Troiano
Copy Editor: Jane Phares
Editorial Assistant: Valorie J. Cooper
Indexer: Mary Ann Laurens
Concept Designer: Melissa Jones Clark
Designer: Rita Yerby
Senior Photographers: Jim Bathie; Charles Walton IV, *Southern Living* magazine
Photographers: Ralph Anderson; Tina Evans, J. Savage Gibson, Sylvia Martin, *Southern Living* magazine
Senior Photo Stylists: Kay E. Clarke; Leslie Byars Simpson, *Southern Living* magazine
Photo Stylist: Virginia R. Cravens
Production and Distribution Director: Phillip Lee
Associate Production Manager: Vanessa Cobbs Richardson
Production Assistant: Valerie L. Heard

Our appreciation to the editorial staff of *Southern Living* magazine and to the Southern Progress Corporation
library staff for their contributions to this volume.

Cover: Mint-Chocolate Roulage (recipe on page 44)
Page 1: Old-Fashioned Carrot Cake (recipe on page 25)
Page 2 *(front to back):* Best-Ever Lemon Meringue Pie (recipe on page 130), Coffee Cream Pie (recipe on page 128),
        Raspberry-Sour Cream Pie (recipe on page 133)

Contents

Bring on Dessert!

Sweet endings have been mealtime essentials for generations.
From cakes to pies, mousses to meringues, and fruits to frosty favorites,
you'll find something here to dazzle family and friends.

Make Dessert Special

Whether they're simple or elegant, desserts make the meal complete. To achieve perfect cakes, pastries, and other sweets, you must measure accurately and mix ingredients properly. Use the following tips to ensure your success in making desserts guaranteed to satisfy the most discriminating sweet tooth.

Blue-Ribbon Cakes

• Position oven rack in center of oven, and preheat oven.

• Use the correct pan size.

• Grease cakepans with solid shortening; do not use oil, butter, or margarine. Lightly dust pans with flour. Do not grease pans for sponge-type cakes.

• Let butter or margarine reach room temperature before mixing.

• Do not sift all-purpose flour unless specified. Always sift cake flour before measuring.

• Beat butter or shortening until creamy. Gradually add sugar, and beat well. (Beating may take up to 7 minutes with a standard mixer and longer with a portable mixer.)

• Add only one egg at a time, and beat after each addition just until yellow disappears.

• Add dry and liquid ingredients alternately to creamed mixture, beginning and ending with dry ingredients. Beat after each addition but only until batter is smooth; do not overbeat.

• Use a rubber spatula to scrape the sides and bottom of the bowl often during mixing.

• Arrange cakepans so that they do not touch each other or the sides of the oven. If placed on separate racks, the pans should be staggered to allow air to circulate.

• Keep oven door closed until the minimum baking time has elapsed.

• Test cake for doneness before removing it from the oven. The cake is done when a wooden pick inserted in the center comes out clean or if the cake springs back when lightly touched.

Testing cake for doneness

• Cool layer cakes in pans 10 minutes and tube cakes in pans 15 minutes. Invert cakes onto wire racks to cool completely.

• Cool cake completely before adding filling and frosting. Lightly brush cake to remove loose crumbs.

• Keep frosting off the serving plate by arranging several strips of wax paper around edges of plate before stacking cake layers.

Placing wax paper under cake before frosting

• Place bottom cake layer upside-down on serving plate.

Spread frosting on top of bottom layer, and smooth to sides of cake with a metal spatula. Place top layer of cake right side up.

• Spread sides of cake with a liberal amount of frosting, making decorative swirls. Spread remaining frosting on top of cake, joining frosting at top and sides; again make decorative swirls.

Frosting cake layers

Cake Problems and Causes

If cake falls:
Oven not hot enough
Undermixing
Insufficient baking
Opening oven door during
    baking
Too much leavening, liquid,
    or sugar

If cake peaks in center:
Oven too hot at start of baking
Too much flour
Not enough liquid

If cake sticks to pan:
Cooled in pan too long
Pan not greased and floured
    properly

If cake cracks and falls apart:
Removed from pan too soon
Too much shortening,
    leavening, or sugar

If crust is sticky:
Insufficient baking
Oven not hot enough
Too much sugar

If texture is coarse:
Inadequate mixing or creaming
Oven not hot enough
Too much leavening

If texture is dry:
Overbaking
Overbeaten egg whites
Too much flour or leavening
Not enough shortening or
    sugar

Picture-Perfect Pies

• Cut shortening into flour using a pastry blender or two knives until mixture resembles coarse crumbs.

Cutting shortening into flour with a pastry blender

• Sprinkle cold water, one tablespoon at a time, over flour mixture; stir with a fork just enough to moisten dry ingredients. Add the minimum amount of water that will moisten flour mixture; too much can make pastry tough and soggy.

• Once water is added to flour mixture, don't overwork the dough—the more you handle it, the more gluten will develop, toughening the pastry.

• Shape dough into a ball, cover with plastic wrap, and chill at least 1 hour. Chilling makes dough easier to handle and helps prevent crust from being soggy.

• Roll dough on a lightly floured surface or pastry cloth, using a floured rolling pin cover on the rolling pin. Place chilled dough in the center of the floured surface; flatten dough with the side of your hand. Carefully roll dough from the center to outer edges; do not roll back and forth across dough, as this will stretch it and cause it to shrink during baking.

Rolling dough with a cloth-covered rolling pin

• Roll dough to ⅛-inch thickness and about two inches larger in diameter than the pieplate.

• To transfer pastry to pieplate, carefully fold dough in half and then into quarters. Place point of fold in center of pieplate, and carefully unfold. Try not to pull at dough, as it will stretch.

Transferring pastry to pieplate

• Trim edges of dough, leaving about ½-inch overhang. (Kitchen shears or scissors are easier to use than a knife.) Fold overhanging dough under, pressing firmly against pieplate edge to seal. Flute as desired (see Creative Finishes).

• For best results, use an ovenproof glass pieplate or a dull metal piepan. Shiny metal pans reflect heat and prevent crust from browning.

• When baking a pastry shell without a filling, prick bottom and sides generously before baking. Do not prick shell if it is to be filled.

Pricking bottom of pastry shell

• Cool baked pastries on a wire rack; this will help keep crusts from becoming soggy.

Creative Finishes

Make a spiral fluted crust design by pinching pastry at an angle between your thumb and index finger.

Cut a scalloped edge for pastry shell by rolling the tip of a teaspoon around edge of pastry.

Give pastry a forked design by gently pressing a fork around edge. Dip fork in flour to keep it from sticking to pastry.

Press a twirled rope around edge of pastry shell. Cut pastry strips about ½ inch wide. Moisten edge of shell; twist rope with one hand, while pressing rope with other hand where it joins pastry.

To apply cutouts, moisten edge of pastry shell, and gently press small cutouts around edge; overlap slightly.

To weave a lattice crust, place strips across pie in one direction. Repeat process of alternately folding back every other strip and laying a strip perpendicular to the original strips.

Pastry Problems and Causes

Tough pastry:
Too little fat
Too much water
Too much flour
Overmixing
Kneading the dough

Crumbly crust:
Too little water
Too much fat
Self-rising flour used
Insufficient mixing

Soggy lower crust:
Filling too moist
Oven not hot enough
Too much liquid in pastry

Crust shrinks:
Too much handling
Pastry stretched in pan
Dough uneven in thickness
Rolling dough back and forth
   with rolling pin

Perfect Ice Cream

• Start with the freshest ingredients possible when making the base for ice cream. If recipe contains eggs, be sure to cook the custard over medium heat, stirring constantly, until mixture reaches 160°.

Cooking custard ingredients

• For a creamier texture, chill ice cream mixture at least 4 hours before freezing it. A chilled mixture also will freeze faster.

• Check the manufacturer's instructions for your ice cream machine. Freezers are made of different materials, making a difference in the ice-salt ratio recommended. Most 1-gallon freezers use 3 to 4 cups rock salt and 20 pounds crushed ice (1 cup salt to 6 cups ice).

• Fill freezer container no more than two-thirds full to allow room for expansion. For electric freezers, let the motor run about one minute before adding ice and salt in layers. Hand-turned freezers should be turned about 1 minute to stir the mixture before freezing.

• Do not skimp on ice and salt; both are essential for freezing ice cream. The ice cream freezes because the ice and salt absorb its heat. Ice alone will not freeze ice cream.

• Use the amount of salt called for by the manufacturer. If you use too little salt, the brine will not get cold enough to thoroughly freeze ice cream. If you use too much salt, the ice cream will freeze too quickly, causing large ice crystals to form. Rock salt is usually preferred over table salt because table salt dissolves rapidly.

• When alternately adding ice and salt, make four thick layers of ice and four thin layers of salt, beginning with ice and ending with salt. Add leftover ice and salt as ice melts and when "ripening" ice cream.

• When ice cream is frozen, the crank barely turns (an electric freezer usually shuts off but needs to be unplugged immediately). Churning takes 25 to 35 minutes.

• Before opening ice cream canister, drain water, and remove ice below level of lid. Wipe canister lid, open, and remove the dasher. Pack ice cream down with a spoon. Cover with plastic wrap or foil, and replace lid.

• Let ice cream "ripen" to harden and blend flavors. Pack freezer bucket with ice and salt using 4 parts ice to 1 part salt. (You need more salt here to harden the ice cream.) Wrap well with a towel or newspaper, and let stand 1 to 2 hours.

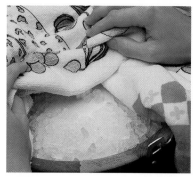

Allowing ice cream to ripen

Ice Cream Shapes

• Freeze commercial or homemade ice cream in special shapes. Select molds with clean lines and simple designs as they are easier to unmold than ones with intricate designs.
• Metal molds conduct cold quickly; this allows for complete freezing and easy unmolding.
• Lightly oil ice cream molds for easy unmolding, or line one-piece molds with plastic wrap.
• Let ice cream soften at room temperature a few minutes before unmolding, or speed up the process by patting the mold with a warm, damp cloth.

Cakes—Plain & Fancy

Birthdays and holidays almost always call for a special cake. Make your next celebration memorable with an easy-to-assemble shortcake, a rich roulage, or a heavenly angel food cake.

Tart Lemon-Cheese Cake, Italian Cream Cake, Devil's Food Cake

Lady Baltimore Cake, Apple Cake with Brown Sugar Glaze, Old South Fruitcake

Lemon-Coconut Cake, Creamy Chocolate Cake, Whipping Cream Pound Cake

Chocolate-Sour Cream Pound Cake, Old-Fashioned Carrot Cake

Banana-Nut Layer Cake (page 24)

White Cake

¾ cup shortening
1½ cups sugar
2¼ cups sifted cake flour
1 tablespoon baking powder
¾ teaspoon salt
1 cup milk
1½ teaspoons vanilla extract
5 egg whites
Favorite Caramel Frosting

Beat shortening at medium speed of an electric mixer until fluffy; gradually add sugar, beating well.

Combine flour, baking powder, and salt; add to shortening mixture alternately with milk, beginning and ending with flour mixture. Beat at low speed until blended after each addition. Stir in vanilla.

Beat egg whites in a large mixing bowl at high speed until stiff peaks form; gently fold into batter. Pour batter into 2 greased and floured 9-inch round cakepans.

Bake at 350° for 25 to 30 minutes or until a wooden pick inserted in center comes out clean. Cool in pans on wire racks 10 minutes; remove from pans, and cool completely on wire racks.

Spread Favorite Caramel Frosting between layers and on sides and top of cake, or frost as desired. **Yield: one 2-layer cake.**

Favorite Caramel Frosting
3 cups sugar, divided
¾ cup milk
1 large egg, beaten
Pinch of salt
½ cup butter or margarine, cut up

Sprinkle ½ cup sugar in a heavy saucepan; place over medium heat. Cook, stirring constantly, until sugar melts and turns a light golden brown.

Combine remaining 2½ cups sugar, milk, egg, and salt, stirring well; stir in butter. Stir into hot caramelized sugar. (Mixture will tend to lump, becoming smooth with further cooking.)

Cook over medium heat, stirring frequently, until a candy thermometer registers 230° (about 15 to 20 minutes). Cool 5 minutes. Beat with a wooden spoon to almost spreading consistency (about 5 minutes), and spread on cooled cake. **Yield: about 2½ cups.**

Yellow Cake

1 cup shortening
2 cups sugar
4 large eggs
3 cups sifted cake flour
2½ teaspoons baking powder
½ teaspoon salt
1 cup milk
1 teaspoon almond extract
1 teaspoon vanilla extract
Pineapple Filling
Seven-Minute Frosting

Beat shortening at medium speed of an electric mixer until fluffy; gradually add sugar, beating well. Add eggs, one at a time, beating until blended after each addition.

Combine flour, baking powder, and salt; add to shortening mixture alternately with milk, beginning and ending with flour mixture. Beat at low speed until blended after each addition. Stir in flavorings. Pour batter into 3 greased and floured 9-inch round cakepans.

Bake at 375° for 20 to 25 minutes or until a wooden pick inserted in center comes out clean. Cool in pans on wire racks 10 minutes; remove from pans, and cool completely on wire racks.

Spread Pineapple Filling between layers; spread Seven-Minute Frosting on sides and top of cake. **Yield: one 3-layer cake.**

Pineapple Filling

3 tablespoons all-purpose flour
½ cup sugar
1 (20-ounce) can crushed pineapple
2 tablespoons butter or margarine

Combine flour and sugar in a small saucepan; add undrained pineapple and butter. Cook over medium heat, stirring constantly, until thickened. Cool. **Yield: 2⅔ cups.**

Seven-Minute Frosting

1½ cups sugar
¼ cup plus 1 tablespoon warm water
2 egg whites
1 tablespoon light corn syrup
Dash of salt
1 teaspoon vanilla extract

Combine first 5 ingredients in top of a large double boiler. Beat at low speed of an electric mixer 30 seconds or just until blended.

Place over boiling water; beat constantly at high speed 7 to 9 minutes or until stiff peaks form and temperature reaches 160°. Remove from heat. Add vanilla; beat 2 minutes or until thick enough to spread. **Yield: 4¼ cups.**

Devil's Food Cake

¾ cup butter or margarine, softened
2 cups sugar
2 large eggs
4 (1-ounce) squares unsweetened chocolate, melted
1 teaspoon vanilla extract
2 cups all-purpose flour
2 teaspoons baking powder
½ teaspoon salt
⅛ teaspoon ground cinnamon (optional)
1½ cups milk
Chocolate Frosting

Beat softened butter at medium speed of an electric mixer until creamy; gradually add sugar, beating well.

Add eggs, one at a time, beating until blended after each addition. Stir in melted chocolate and vanilla.

Combine flour, baking powder, salt, and, if desired, cinnamon; add to chocolate mixture alternately with milk, beginning and ending with flour mixture. Beat at low speed until blended after each addition. Pour batter into 2 greased and floured 9-inch round cakepans.

Bake at 350° for 25 to 30 minutes or until a wooden pick inserted in center comes out clean. Cool in pans on wire racks 10 minutes; remove from pans, and cool completely on wire racks.

Spread Chocolate Frosting between layers and on sides and top of cake. **Yield: one 2-layer cake.**

Chocolate Frosting

4½ (1-ounce) squares unsweetened chocolate
½ cup butter or margarine
5⅔ cups sifted powdered sugar
½ cup milk
1 teaspoon vanilla extract

Combine chocolate and butter in a heavy saucepan; cook over low heat until chocolate melts. Remove from heat, and cool.

Add powdered sugar and milk; beat at low speed of an electric mixer until smooth. Stir in vanilla. **Yield: 3 cups.**

Creamy Chocolate Cake

Creamy Chocolate Cake

1 (4-ounce) package sweet baking chocolate
½ cup boiling water
1 cup butter or margarine, softened
2 cups sugar
4 large eggs
1 teaspoon baking soda
1 cup buttermilk
3¾ cups sifted cake flour
½ teaspoon salt
2 teaspoons vanilla extract
Buttercream Filling
Creamy Frosting
1 cup finely chopped pecans
Garnish: pecan halves

Grease three 9-inch round cakepans, and line with wax paper; grease and flour paper. Set aside.

Combine chocolate and boiling water; stir until chocolate melts. Set aside.

Beat butter at medium speed of an electric mixer until creamy. Add sugar; beat 5 minutes. Add eggs, one at a time, beating after each addition.

Dissolve soda in buttermilk. Combine flour and salt; add to butter mixture alternately with buttermilk mixture, beginning and ending with flour mixture. Beat at low speed until blended after each addition. Stir in chocolate and vanilla. Pour batter into prepared pans.

Bake at 350° for 30 minutes or until a wooden pick inserted in center comes out clean. Remove from pans. Remove wax paper; cool on wire racks.

Spread filling between layers; spread frosting on sides and top of cake. Decorate top of cake, using a cake comb, if desired. Press chopped pecans into frosting on sides of cake. Garnish, if desired. **Yield: one 3-layer cake.**

Buttercream Filling

⅓ cup unsalted butter, softened
2¼ cups sifted powdered sugar
2 to 3 tablespoons half-and-half

Beat butter at medium speed of an electric mixer until creamy; gradually add sugar, beating well. Add half-and-half, 1 tablespoon at a time, beating until spreading consistency. **Yield: 1⅓ cups.**

Creamy Frosting

¾ cup sugar
⅓ cup water
3 egg yolks
1 cup unsalted butter, softened
2 (1-ounce) squares unsweetened chocolate, melted and cooled
2 (1-ounce) squares semisweet chocolate, melted and cooled
1 teaspoon chocolate extract

Combine sugar and water in a medium saucepan. Bring to a boil; cook over medium heat, without stirring, until mixture reaches soft ball stage (240°).

Beat egg yolks at high speed of an electric mixer until thick and pale; continue beating, adding 240° syrup in a heavy stream. Beat until mixture thickens and cools.

Add butter, 3 tablespoons at a time, beating until smooth. Stir in melted chocolate and extract. Chill to spreadable consistency. **Yield: 2 cups.**

Creamy Chocolate Cake Technique

Add texture to a frosted cake by decorating with a frosting comb (available in kitchen shops).

Lemon-Coconut Cake

1 cup butter, softened
2 cups sugar
3¼ cups sifted cake flour
2½ teaspoons baking powder
½ teaspoon salt
1 cup milk
¾ teaspoon coconut extract
½ teaspoon lemon extract
6 egg whites
¾ teaspoon cream of tartar
Lemon-Coconut Filling
Fluffy Lemon Frosting
1½ to 2 cups flaked coconut
Garnish: lemon rind curls

Beat softened butter at medium speed of an electric mixer until creamy; gradually add sugar, beating well.

Combine flour, baking powder, and salt; add to butter mixture alternately with milk, beginning and ending with flour mixture. Beat mixture at low speed until blended after each addition. Stir in flavorings.

Beat egg whites in a large mixing bowl at high speed until foamy. Add cream of tartar; beat until stiff peaks form. Gently fold one-third of egg whites into batter; fold in remaining egg whites. Pour batter into 3 greased and floured 9-inch round cakepans.

Bake at 350° for 20 to 25 minutes or until a wooden pick inserted in center comes out clean. Cool in pans on wire racks 10 minutes; remove from pans, and cool completely on wire racks.

Spread Lemon-Coconut Filling between layers; spread Fluffy Lemon Frosting on sides and top of cake. Gently press coconut into frosting. Garnish, if desired. **Yield: one 3-layer cake.**

Lemon-Coconut Filling

1 cup sugar
3 tablespoons cornstarch
⅛ teaspoon salt
1 tablespoon grated lemon rind
⅔ cup lemon juice
⅓ cup water
5 egg yolks, beaten
½ cup butter or margarine
½ cup flaked coconut

Combine first 3 ingredients in a heavy saucepan; stir well.

Stir in lemon rind, juice, and water. Cook over medium heat, stirring constantly, until mixture thickens and comes to a boil. Boil 1 minute, stirring constantly.

Stir half of hot mixture gradually into egg yolks; add to remaining hot mixture, stirring constantly. Cook 1 minute, stirring constantly.

Remove from heat; add butter and coconut, stirring until butter melts. Cool completely. **Yield: 2½ cups.**

Fluffy Lemon Frosting

1 cup sugar
⅓ cup water
2 tablespoons light corn syrup
2 egg whites
¼ cup sifted powdered sugar
1 teaspoon grated lemon rind
½ teaspoon lemon extract

Combine first 3 ingredients in a heavy saucepan. Cook over medium heat, stirring constantly, until clear. Cook, without stirring, until candy thermometer registers 232°.

Beat egg whites at high speed of an electric mixer until soft peaks form; continue to beat, adding hot syrup mixture. Add powdered sugar, lemon rind, and lemon extract; continue beating until stiff peaks form and frosting is spreading consistency. **Yield: about 3 cups.**

Lemon-Coconut Cake

Tart Lemon-Cheese Cake

1 cup butter, softened
2 cups sugar
¾ cup water
¼ cup milk
3¼ cups sifted cake flour
2¾ teaspoons baking powder
½ teaspoon salt
½ teaspoon rum flavoring or 1 teaspoon
    vanilla extract
6 egg whites
Lemon-Cheese Filling
Lemony White Frosting

Beat butter at medium speed of an electric mixer until creamy; gradually add sugar, beating well.

Combine water and milk; set aside.

Combine flour, baking powder, and salt; add to butter mixture alternately with milk mixture, beginning and ending with flour mixture. Stir in rum flavoring.

Beat egg whites in a large mixing bowl at high speed until stiff peaks form; fold into batter. Pour batter into 3 greased and floured 9-inch round cakepans.

Bake at 350° for 20 to 25 minutes or until a wooden pick inserted in center comes out clean. Cool in pans on wire racks 10 minutes; remove from pans, and cool completely on wire racks.

Spread Lemon-Cheese Filling between layers and on top of cake. Spread Lemony White Frosting on sides. **Yield: one 3-layer cake.**

Lemon-Cheese Filling

1 cup sugar
3 tablespoons cornstarch
⅛ teaspoon salt
2 tablespoons grated lemon rind
1 cup lemon juice
6 egg yolks, beaten
⅓ cup butter or margarine

Combine first 3 ingredients in a heavy saucepan; stir well. Add lemon rind and juice; cook over medium heat, stirring constantly, until mixture thickens and comes to a boil. Boil 1 minute, stirring constantly.

Stir half of hot mixture gradually into egg yolks; add to remaining hot mixture, stirring constantly. Cook, stirring constantly, about 1 minute or until mixture is thoroughly heated.

Remove from heat. Add butter, stirring until butter melts; cool. **Yield: 2 cups.**

Lemony White Frosting

1 cup sugar
⅓ cup water
2 tablespoons light corn syrup
2 egg whites
¼ cup sifted powdered sugar
½ teaspoon lemon extract

Combine first 3 ingredients in a heavy saucepan. Cook over medium heat, stirring constantly, until clear. Cook, without stirring, until candy thermometer registers 232°.

Beat egg whites at high speed of an electric mixer until soft peaks form; continue to beat, adding hot syrup mixture.

Add powdered sugar and lemon extract; continue beating until stiff peaks form and frosting is spreading consistency. **Yield: about 3 cups.**

Why Use Cake Flour?

Cake flour is a soft wheat flour with a high starch content. It makes very tender, fine-textured cakes but should be sifted before measuring. The substitution for 1 cup cake flour is 1 cup all-purpose flour minus 2 tablespoons.

Italian Cream Cake

Italian Cream Cake

1 cup butter or margarine, softened
2 cups sugar
5 large eggs, separated
2½ cups all-purpose flour
1 teaspoon baking soda
1 cup milk
⅔ cup finely chopped pecans
1 (3½-ounce) can flaked coconut
1 teaspoon vanilla extract
½ teaspoon cream of tartar
3 tablespoons light rum
Cream Cheese Frosting

   Grease three 9-inch round cakepans, and line with wax paper; grease and flour paper. Set aside.
   Beat butter at medium speed of an electric mixer until creamy; add sugar, beating well. Add egg yolks, one at a time, beating until blended after each addition.

   Combine flour and baking soda; add to butter mixture alternately with milk, beginning and ending with flour mixture. Beat at low speed after each addition. Stir in chopped pecans, coconut, and vanilla.
   Beat egg whites in a large mixing bowl at high speed until foamy. Add cream of tartar; beat until stiff peaks form. Gently fold one-third of egg whites into batter; fold in remaining egg whites. Pour batter into prepared pans.
   Bake at 350° for 25 to 30 minutes or until a wooden pick inserted in center comes out clean. Cool in pans on wire racks 10 minutes. Remove from pans; peel off wax paper, and cool completely on wire racks.
   Sprinkle each layer with 1 tablespoon light rum. Let stand 10 minutes. Spread Cream Cheese Frosting between layers and on sides and top of cake. **Yield: one 3-layer cake.**

Cream Cheese Frosting
1 (8-ounce) package cream cheese, softened
½ cup butter, softened
1 (16-ounce) package powdered sugar, sifted
1 cup chopped pecans
2 teaspoons vanilla extract

   Combine cream cheese and butter, beating until smooth. Gradually add powdered sugar, and beat until light and fluffy. Stir in pecans and vanilla. **Yield: 4 cups.**

From left: Lady Baltimore Cake and Lord Baltimore Cake

Lord Baltimore Cake

¾ cup shortening
2¼ cups sugar
8 egg yolks
3¾ cups sifted cake flour
1½ tablespoons baking powder
½ teaspoon salt
1¾ cups milk
½ teaspoon almond extract
½ teaspoon vanilla extract
Frosting
1 cup chopped mixed candied fruit
1 cup chopped pecans or walnuts
½ cup macaroon crumbs
1 teaspoon vanilla extract
½ teaspoon almond extract
Garnish: candied cherries

Beat shortening at medium speed of an electric mixer until fluffy; gradually add sugar, beating well. Add egg yolks, one at a time, beating until blended after each addition.

Combine flour, baking powder, and salt; add to shortening mixture alternately with milk, beginning and ending with flour mixture. Beat at low speed until blended after each addition. Stir in ½ teaspoon each of almond and vanilla extract. Pour batter into 3 greased and floured 9-inch round cakepans.

Bake at 350° for 20 to 25 minutes or until a wooden pick inserted in center comes out clean. Cool in pans on wire racks 10 minutes. Remove from pans, and cool completely on wire racks.

Combine 2 cups Frosting, candied fruit, and

next 4 ingredients; spread between layers. Spread remaining Frosting on sides and top of cake. Garnish, if desired. **Yield: one 3-layer cake.**

Frosting

1½ cups sugar
½ cup water
1 tablespoon light corn syrup
4 egg whites

Combine first 3 ingredients in a heavy saucepan; cook over low heat until mixture reaches soft ball stage (240°).

Beat egg whites in a large mixing bowl at high speed until soft peaks form; continue beating, adding 240° syrup mixture. Beat 1 minute. **Yield: 7 cups.**

Lady Baltimore Cake

1 cup butter or margarine, softened
2 cups sugar
½ cup water
½ cup milk
3 cups sifted cake flour
2¾ teaspoons baking powder
½ teaspoon salt
½ teaspoon almond extract
6 egg whites
1 cup chopped raisins or currants
1 cup chopped dried figs
1 cup chopped almonds or walnuts
½ cup sherry or brandy
Boiled Frosting
Garnish: whole roasted almonds

Beat softened butter at medium speed of an electric mixer until creamy; gradually add sugar, beating well.

Combine water and milk; set aside.

Combine flour, baking powder, and salt; add to butter mixture alternately with milk mixture,

beginning and ending with flour mixture. Beat at low speed until blended after each addition. Stir in almond extract.

Beat egg whites in a large mixing bowl at high speed until stiff peaks form; fold into batter. Pour batter into 3 greased and floured 9-inch round cakepans.

Bake at 350° for 25 minutes or until a wooden pick inserted in center comes out clean. Cool in pans on wire racks 10 minutes; remove from pans, and cool completely on wire racks.

Combine raisins, figs, almonds, and sherry; let stand 30 minutes. Drain well, discarding sherry; set fruit aside.

Combine 2 cups Boiled Frosting and fruit mixture; spread between layers. Spread remaining frosting on sides and top of cake. Garnish, if desired. **Yield: one 3-layer cake.**

Boiled Frosting

1½ cups sugar
½ teaspoon cream of tartar
⅛ teaspoon salt
½ cup water
4 egg whites
½ teaspoon almond extract
½ teaspoon vanilla extract

Combine first 4 ingredients in a heavy saucepan. Cook over medium heat, stirring constantly, until clear. Cook, without stirring, to soft ball stage (240°).

Beat egg whites in a large mixing bowl at high speed until soft peaks form; continue beating, adding 240° syrup mixture. Add flavorings; beat until stiff peaks form and frosting is spreading consistency. **Yield: 7 cups.**

Apple Cake with Brown Sugar Glaze

2 cups sugar
1 cup vegetable oil
3 large eggs
3 cups all-purpose flour
1 teaspoon baking soda
½ teaspoon salt
1 teaspoon ground cinnamon
3 cups peeled, finely chopped cooking apple
½ cup chopped pecans
Brown Sugar Glaze

Beat first 3 ingredients at medium speed of an electric mixer until creamy.

Combine flour and next 3 ingredients; add to sugar mixture, beating well. Stir in apple and pecans. Spoon batter into a greased and floured 12-cup Bundt pan.

Bake at 350° for 1 hour and 20 minutes or until a wooden pick inserted in center comes out clean. Cool in pan on a wire rack 10 to 15 minutes; remove from pan, and cool completely on wire rack.

Drizzle Brown Sugar Glaze over cake. **Yield: one 10-inch cake.**

Brown Sugar Glaze
½ cup firmly packed brown sugar
¼ cup butter or margarine
2 tablespoons evaporated milk

Combine all ingredients in a small saucepan; cook over high heat, stirring constantly, 2 minutes or until butter melts. Cool to lukewarm. **Yield: ½ cup.**

Favorite Stack Cake

½ cup butter or margarine, softened
1 cup sugar
½ cup buttermilk
1 large egg
1 teaspoon vanilla extract
3½ cups all-purpose flour
1½ teaspoons baking powder
½ teaspoon baking soda
½ teaspoon salt
¼ cup butter or margarine, melted
Dried Apple Filling
Sifted powdered sugar (optional)

Beat butter at medium speed of an electric mixer until creamy; add sugar, beating well. Add buttermilk, egg, and vanilla; beat until blended.

Combine flour, baking powder, soda, and salt; gradually add to butter mixture, beating until blended.

Divide dough into 6 equal portions; pat each into the bottom of a lightly greased 9-inch round cakepan. Prick dough several times with a fork.

Bake at 400° for 10 minutes or until lightly browned. Remove layers to a wire rack; cool.

Stack cake layers, spreading melted butter and Dried Apple Filling between each layer. Cover and chill 8 hours before serving. Sprinkle with powdered sugar, if desired. **Yield: one 9-inch cake.**

Dried Apple Filling
2 (8-ounce) packages dried apples
4 cups water
¾ cup sugar
1 teaspoon ground cinnamon
½ teaspoon pumpkin pie spice

Combine apples and water in a large saucepan. Bring to a boil; cover, reduce heat, and simmer 30 minutes or until tender. Add sugar and spices; stir well. **Yield: about 3½ cups.**

Hummingbird Cake

Hummingbird Cake

3 cups all-purpose flour
1 teaspoon baking soda
½ teaspoon salt
2 cups sugar
1 teaspoon ground cinnamon
3 large eggs, lightly beaten
¾ cup vegetable oil
1½ teaspoons vanilla extract
1 (8-ounce) can crushed pineapple, undrained
1 cup chopped pecans
1¾ cups mashed banana
Cream Cheese Frosting
Garnish: fresh rose petals

Combine first 5 ingredients in a large bowl; add eggs and oil, stirring until dry ingredients are moistened. (Do not beat.)

Stir in vanilla and next 3 ingredients. Pour batter into 3 greased and floured 9-inch round cakepans.

Bake at 350° for 23 to 28 minutes or until a wooden pick inserted in center comes out clean. Cool in pans on wire racks 10 minutes; remove from pans, and cool completely on wire racks.

Spread Cream Cheese Frosting between layers and on sides and top of cake. Store in refrigerator up to 3 days, or freeze up to 3 months. Garnish, if desired. **Yield: one 3-layer cake.**

Cream Cheese Frosting
½ cup butter or margarine, softened
1 (8-ounce) package cream cheese, softened
1 (16-ounce) package powdered sugar, sifted
1 teaspoon vanilla extract

Beat butter and cream cheese at medium speed of an electric mixer until creamy. Gradually add powdered sugar, beating until light and fluffy. Stir in vanilla. **Yield: about 3 cups.**

Note: Store cake in the refrigerator.

Banana-Nut Layer Cake

(pictured on page 11)

½ cup butter or margarine, softened
¾ cup sugar
¾ cup firmly packed brown sugar
2 large eggs, separated
1 teaspoon baking soda
⅓ cup buttermilk
2 cups all-purpose flour
½ teaspoon ground allspice
½ teaspoon instant coffee granules
3 ripe bananas, mashed
1 cup chopped pecans, toasted
1 teaspoon vanilla extract
Vanilla Buttercream Frosting
Garnish: toasted sliced almonds

Beat butter at medium speed of an electric mixer until creamy; gradually add sugars, beating well. Add egg yolks, beating until blended.

Dissolve soda in buttermilk. Combine flour, allspice, and coffee granules; add to butter mixture alternately with buttermilk mixture, beginning and ending with flour mixture. Beat at low speed until blended after each addition. Stir in mashed banana, pecans, and vanilla.

Beat egg whites at high speed until stiff peaks form; gently fold into batter, one-third at a time. Pour batter into 2 greased and floured 8-inch round cakepans.

Bake at 350° for 30 minutes or until a wooden pick inserted in center comes out clean. Cool in pans on wire racks 10 minutes; remove from pans, and cool completely on wire racks.

Split cake layers in half horizontally to make 4 layers. Set aside 1½ cups Vanilla Buttercream Frosting. Spread remaining 3 cups frosting between layers and on sides and top of cake.

Spoon 1 cup reserved frosting into a decorating bag fitted with a No. 2B tip. Pipe frosting in a lattice design across top of cake. Spoon remaining ½ cup reserved frosting into a bag fitted with

a No. 21 tip, and pipe frosting around top edge of cake. Garnish, if desired. **Yield: one 4-layer cake.**

Vanilla Buttercream Frosting

2¼ cups butter or margarine, softened
6 cups sifted powdered sugar
3 tablespoons milk
1½ teaspoons vanilla extract
¾ teaspoon ground allspice

Beat butter at medium speed of an electric mixer until creamy; add sugar, beating until light and fluffy. Add milk; beat until spreading consistency. Stir in vanilla and allspice. **Yield: 4½ cups.**

Special Spice Cake

1 cup butter or margarine, softened
2 cups firmly packed light brown sugar
3 large eggs
1 teaspoon baking soda
1 cup buttermilk
2 cups all-purpose flour
2 teaspoons ground cinnamon
1 teaspoon vanilla extract
½ cup golden raisins
½ cup raisins
1 cup chopped pecans
Chocolate-Coffee Frosting

Beat butter at medium speed of an electric mixer until creamy; gradually add sugar, beating well. Add eggs, one at a time, beating until blended after each addition.

Dissolve soda in buttermilk. Combine flour and cinnamon; add to butter mixture alternately with buttermilk mixture, beginning and ending with flour mixture. Beat at low speed until blended after each addition. Stir in vanilla, raisins, and pecans. Pour batter into 3 greased and floured 9-inch round cakepans.

Bake at 325° for 25 to 27 minutes or until a

wooden pick inserted in center comes out clean. Cool in pans on wire racks 10 minutes; remove from pans, and cool completely on wire racks.

Spread Chocolate-Coffee Frosting between layers and on sides and top of cake. **Yield: one 3-layer cake.**

Chocolate-Coffee Frosting

1 teaspoon instant coffee granules
½ cup boiling water
7 cups sifted powdered sugar
⅔ cup cocoa
½ cup butter or margarine, softened
1 teaspoon vanilla extract

Dissolve coffee granules in boiling water, and set aside.

Combine powdered sugar and cocoa; mix well. Set aside.

Beat butter at medium speed of an electric mixer until creamy; add sugar mixture and vanilla. Gradually add coffee mixture, beating at high speed to desired spreading consistency. **Yield: enough for one 3-layer cake.**

Old-Fashioned Carrot Cake

3 cups shredded carrot
2 cups all-purpose flour
1 teaspoon baking soda
1 teaspoon baking powder
½ teaspoon salt
2 cups sugar
1 teaspoon ground cinnamon
4 large eggs, beaten
¾ cup vegetable oil
1 teaspoon vanilla extract
Cream Cheese Frosting
Garnish: chopped pecans

Grease three 9-inch round cakepans; line with wax paper. Grease and flour paper. Set aside.

Combine first 7 ingredients in a large bowl; add eggs, oil, and vanilla, stirring until blended. Pour into prepared pans.

Bake at 350° for 25 minutes or until a wooden pick inserted in center comes out clean. Cool in pans on wire racks 10 minutes; remove from pans, and cool completely on wire racks.

Spread Cream Cheese Frosting between layers and on sides and top of cake. Garnish, if desired, and chill. Freeze up to 3 months, if desired. **Yield: one 3-layer cake.**

Cream Cheese Frosting

1 (8-ounce) package cream cheese, softened
½ cup butter or margarine, softened
1 (16-ounce) package powdered sugar, sifted
1 teaspoon vanilla extract

Beat cream cheese and butter at medium speed of an electric mixer until creamy. Gradually add powdered sugar, beating until light and fluffy. Stir in vanilla. **Yield: about 3 cups.**

Old-Fashioned Carrot Cake

Old South Fruitcake

Old South Fruitcake

1½ cups butter, softened
1¼ cups firmly packed brown sugar
⅓ cup molasses
7 large eggs, separated
3 cups all-purpose flour
1½ pounds yellow, green, and red candied
    pineapple, chopped (about 3¾ cups)
1 pound red and green candied cherries,
    halved (about 2½ cups)
3 cups pecan halves, lightly toasted
1 cup walnuts, coarsely chopped
¾ cup golden raisins
¾ cup raisins
½ cup all-purpose flour
1 teaspoon ground allspice
¼ cup brandy
1 tablespoon powdered sugar
Additional brandy (optional)

Draw a circle with a 10-inch diameter on a piece of brown paper, using a tube pan as a guide. (Do not use recycled paper.) Cut out circle; set tube pan insert in center, and draw around inside tube. Cut out smaller circle. Grease paper, and set aside.

Grease heavily and flour 10-inch tube pan, and set aside.

Beat butter at medium speed of an electric mixer; gradually add brown sugar, beating well. Stir in molasses.

Beat egg yolks; alternately add yolks and 3 cups flour to butter mixture. Beat until blended. (Batter will be very thick.)

Combine pineapple, cherries, nuts, and raisins in a bowl; sprinkle with ½ cup flour and allspice, stirring to coat well. Stir mixture into batter.

Beat egg whites in a large bowl at high speed until stiff peaks form; gradually fold into batter.

Spoon batter into prepared pan. Cover pan with 10-inch paper circle, greased side down.

Bake at 250° for 4 hours or until a wooden pick inserted in center comes out clean. Remove from oven; discard paper cover. Loosen cake from sides of pan, using a narrow metal spatula; invert pan, and remove cake. Invert cake again onto a wire rack.

Combine ¼ cup brandy and powdered sugar; stir well. Slowly pour brandy evenly over cake; cool completely on wire rack.

Wrap cake in brandy-soaked cheesecloth. Store in an airtight container in a cool place 3 weeks. Pour a small amount of brandy over cake each week, if desired. **Yield: one 10-inch cake.**

Note: Refrigerate Old South Fruitcake for longer storage. Refrigeration also makes slicing the cake neater and easier.

Variation

Old South Fruitcake Loaves: Spoon batter into 3 greased and floured 8½- x 4½- x 3-inch loafpans or 6 greased and floured 6- x 3½- x 2¼-inch miniature loafpans. Bake at 250° for 2½ hours or until cakes test done.

Old South Fruitcake Technique

Soak cheesecloth in brandy; wring out excess moisture. Wrap fruitcake in cheesecloth to keep it moist and flavorful.

Smoothest Southern Pound Cake

1 **cup butter or margarine, softened**
3 **cups sugar**
3 **cups sifted cake flour**
¼ **teaspoon baking soda**
6 **large eggs, separated**
1 **(8-ounce) carton sour cream**
1 **teaspoon vanilla extract**

Beat butter at medium speed of an electric mixer (not a hand-held one) 2 minutes or until butter is creamy. Gradually add sugar, beating 5 to 7 minutes.

Combine flour and soda; add to butter mixture 1 cup at a time. (Batter will be extremely thick.)

Add egg yolks to batter, and mix well. Stir in sour cream and vanilla. Beat egg whites in a large mixing bowl at high speed until stiff; fold into batter. Spoon batter into a greased and floured 10-inch Bundt or tube pan.

Bake at 300° for 2 hours or until a wooden pick inserted in center comes out clean. (You may also spoon batter into two 9- x 5- x 3-inch loafpans, and bake at 300° for 1½ hours or until a wooden pick inserted in center comes out clean.)

Cool in pan on a wire rack 10 to 15 minutes; remove from pan, and cool completely on wire rack. **Yield: one 10-inch cake or two loaves.**

Variation

If you prefer to use a hand-held mixer or prefer not to separate the eggs, try this procedure.

Beat butter at medium speed of an electric mixer about 2 minutes or until creamy. Gradually add sugar, beating 7 minutes. Add eggs, one at a time, beating just until yellow disappears.

Combine flour and soda; add to butter mixture alternately with sour cream, beginning and ending with flour mixture. Beat at low speed just until blended after each addition. Stir in vanilla.

Bake as directed.

Whipping Cream Pound Cake

1 **cup butter or margarine, softened**
3 **cups sugar**
6 **large eggs**
3 **cups sifted cake flour**
1 **cup whipping cream**
2 **teaspoons vanilla extract**
Powdered sugar
Garnish: fresh strawberries, mint sprigs

Beat butter at medium speed of an electric mixer 2 minutes or until creamy. Gradually add 3 cups sugar, beating 5 to 7 minutes.

Add eggs, one at a time, beating just until yellow disappears.

Add flour to butter mixture alternately with whipping cream, beginning and ending with flour. Beat at low speed just until blended after each addition. Stir in vanilla. Spoon batter into a greased and floured 10-inch Bundt pan.

Bake at 325° for 1 hour or until a wooden pick inserted in center comes out clean. Cool in pan on a wire rack 10 minutes; remove from pan, and cool completely on wire rack.

Sift powdered sugar over cake. Garnish, if desired. **Yield: one 10-inch cake.**

Whipping Cream Pound Cake Technique

Sift powdered sugar over cooled pound cake; place wax paper underneath wire rack to catch excess sugar.

Whipping Cream Pound Cake

Cream Cheese Pound Cake

1½ cups butter, softened
1 (8-ounce) package cream cheese, softened
3 cups sugar
6 large eggs
1½ teaspoons vanilla extract
3 cups all-purpose flour
⅛ teaspoon salt

Beat butter and cream cheese at medium speed of an electric mixer 2 minutes or until mixture is creamy. Gradually add sugar, beating 5 to 7 minutes.

Add eggs, one at a time, beating just until yellow disappears. Add vanilla, mixing well.

Combine flour and salt; gradually add to butter mixture, beating at low speed just until blended after each addition. Spoon batter into a greased and floured 10-inch tube pan.

Fill a 2-cup, ovenproof measuring cup with water, and place in oven with tube pan.

Bake at 300° for 1 hour and 45 minutes or until a wooden pick inserted in center comes out clean. Cool in pan on a wire rack 10 to 15 minutes; remove from pan, and cool completely on wire rack. **Yield: one 10-inch cake.**

Chocolate-Sour Cream Pound Cake

1 cup butter or margarine, softened
2 cups sugar
1 cup firmly packed brown sugar
6 large eggs
2½ cups all-purpose flour
¼ teaspoon baking soda
½ cup cocoa
1 (8-ounce) carton sour cream
2 teaspoons vanilla extract
Powdered sugar (optional)

Beat butter at medium speed of an electric mixer 2 minutes or until creamy. Gradually add sugars, beating 5 to 7 minutes.

Add eggs, one at a time, beating just until yellow disappears.

Combine flour, baking soda, and cocoa; add to butter mixture alternately with sour cream, beginning and ending with flour mixture. Beat at low speed just until blended after each addition. Stir in vanilla. Spoon batter into a greased and floured 10-inch tube pan.

Bake at 325° for 1 hour and 20 minutes or until a wooden pick inserted in center comes out clean. Cool in pan on a wire rack 10 to 15 minutes; remove from pan, and cool completely on wire rack. Sprinkle with powdered sugar, if desired. **Yield: one 10-inch cake.**

Chocolate-Sour Cream Pound Cake

Orange-Pecan Pound Cake

1 cup butter or margarine, softened
1 cup sugar
3 large eggs
1½ teaspoons grated orange rind
½ teaspoon grated lemon rind
¼ teaspoon orange extract
½ cup finely chopped pecans
2 cups all-purpose flour, divided
½ teaspoon baking powder
⅛ teaspoon salt
⅓ cup milk

Beat butter at medium speed of an electric mixer 2 minutes or until creamy. Gradually add sugar, beating 5 to 7 minutes.

Add eggs, one at a time, beating just until yellow disappears. Stir in rinds and orange extract.

Combine pecans and ¼ cup flour; set aside.

Combine remaining 1¾ cups flour, baking powder, and salt; add to butter mixture alternately with milk, beginning and ending with flour mixture. Beat at low speed just until blended after each addition.

Stir in floured pecans. Spoon batter into a greased and floured 9- x 5- x 3-inch loafpan.

Bake at 325° for 1 hour and 5 minutes or until a wooden pick inserted in center comes out clean. Cool in pan on a wire rack 10 to 15 minutes; remove from pan, and cool completely on wire rack. **Yield: 1 loaf.**

Peach Brandy Pound Cake

1 cup butter or margarine, softened
3 cups sugar
6 large eggs
3 cups all-purpose flour
¼ teaspoon baking soda
⅛ teaspoon salt
1 (8-ounce) carton sour cream
½ cup peach brandy
2 teaspoons rum
1 teaspoon orange extract
1 teaspoon vanilla extract
½ teaspoon lemon extract
¼ teaspoon almond extract

Beat butter at medium speed of an electric mixer 2 minutes or until creamy. Gradually add sugar, beating 5 minutes.

Add eggs, one at a time, beating just until yellow disappears.

Combine flour, soda, and salt; add to butter mixture alternately with sour cream, beginning and ending with flour mixture. Beat at low speed just until blended after each addition. Stir in brandy and remaining ingredients. Spoon batter into a greased and floured 10-inch tube pan.

Bake at 325° for 1½ hours or until a wooden pick inserted in center comes out clean. Cool in pan on a wire rack 10 to 15 minutes; remove from pan, and cool completely on wire rack. **Yield: one 10-inch cake.**

Pound Cake Pointers

- Use the correct pan size. Recipes suitable for a 10-inch tube pan, which holds 16 cups, won't always fit in a 12- or 13-cup Bundt pan.
- Grease pan with solid shortening; do not substitute butter, margarine, or vegetable cooking spray. Flour the greased pan.
- Beat butter and sugar 5 to 7 minutes or until mixture is a fluffy consistency.
- Keep oven door closed until minimum baking time has elapsed.

Angel Food Cake

12 egg whites
1½ teaspoons cream of tartar
¼ teaspoon salt
1½ cups sugar
1 cup sifted cake flour
1½ teaspoons vanilla extract

Beat egg whites in a large mixing bowl at high speed of an electric mixer until foamy. Add cream of tartar and salt; beat until soft peaks form. Add sugar, 2 tablespoons at a time, beating until stiff peaks form.

Sprinkle flour over egg white mixture, ¼ cup at a time; fold in carefully. Fold in vanilla. Spoon batter into an ungreased 10-inch tube pan, spreading evenly.

Bake at 375° for 30 to 35 minutes or until cake springs back when lightly touched. Invert pan, and cool 40 minutes. Loosen cake from sides of pan using a narrow metal spatula; remove from pan. **Yield: one 10-inch cake.**

Variation

Chocolate Angel Food Cake: For a chocolate version, sift ¼ cup cocoa with flour.

Angel Cake Surprise

1 (10-inch) angel food cake
½ cup semisweet chocolate morsels
3 cups whipping cream, divided
1 tablespoon Chambord or other raspberry-
    flavored liqueur
¼ cup sifted powdered sugar
Garnishes: grated chocolate, fresh raspberries

Slice off top one-third of cake; set aside. Using a sharp knife, hollow out center of remaining cake, leaving a 1-inch shell; reserve cake pieces

for another use. Place cake shell on serving plate, and set aside.

Melt chocolate morsels in a heavy saucepan over low heat, stirring occasionally, until smooth; remove from heat, and cool.

Beat 1 cup whipping cream at medium speed of an electric mixer until firm peaks form; fold in liqueur and melted chocolate. Spoon into cake shell; place top one-third of cake over filling, pressing firmly.

Beat remaining 2 cups whipping cream at medium speed until foamy; add powdered sugar, beating until firm peaks form. Spread over sides and top of cake; chill up to 8 hours. Garnish, if desired. **Yield: one 10-inch cake.**

Note: You may substitute 1 tablespoon Cointreau or other orange-flavored liqueur for Chambord.

Triple Mint Ice Cream Angel Dessert

1 (10-inch) angel food cake
4 cups chocolate-mint ice cream, slightly
    softened and divided
2 cups pink peppermint ice cream, slightly
    softened
Whipped Cream Frosting
Chocolate-Mint Sauce

Split cake horizontally into 4 equal layers. Place bottom layer on a serving plate; spread top of layer with half of chocolate-mint ice cream to within ½ inch from edge. Top with second cake layer; cover and freeze 45 minutes or until firm.

Spread second cake layer with pink peppermint ice cream. Add third cake layer; cover and freeze 45 minutes or until firm.

Spread third layer with remaining chocolate-mint ice cream, and top with remaining cake layer; cover and freeze until firm.

Triple Mint Ice Cream Angel Dessert

Spread Whipped Cream Frosting on sides and top of cake. Cover and freeze up to 12 hours, if desired; let stand at room temperature 15 to 20 minutes before serving. Serve with Chocolate-Mint Sauce. **Yield: one 10-inch cake.**

Whipped Cream Frosting
3 cups whipping cream
3 tablespoons powdered sugar
1½ teaspoons vanilla extract

Beat whipping cream at low speed of an electric mixer until thickened; add sugar and vanilla, beating until firm peaks form. **Yield: 6 cups.**

Chocolate-Mint Sauce
¾ cup half-and-half
1 (10-ounce) package mint chocolate morsels
1½ cups miniature marshmallows
¼ teaspoon salt
1 teaspoon vanilla extract

Heat half-and-half in a heavy saucepan over low heat. Stir in chocolate morsels, marshmallows, and salt; cook, stirring constantly, until chocolate and marshmallows melt. Remove from heat; stir in vanilla. **Yield: 1½ cups.**

Note: Dip knife in hot water to make cutting cake easier.

Daffodil Sponge Cake

Daffodil Sponge Cake

1 cup sifted cake flour
½ cup sugar
4 egg yolks
½ teaspoon lemon extract
10 egg whites
1 teaspoon cream of tartar
½ teaspoon salt
¾ cup sugar
½ teaspoon vanilla extract
Lemon Glaze
Garnishes: lemon roses, fresh lemon balm
    leaves

   Sift flour and ½ cup sugar together 3 times; set aside.
   Beat egg yolks at high speed of an electric mixer 4 minutes or until thick and pale. Add lemon extract; beat at medium speed 5 minutes or until thick. Set aside.
   Beat egg whites, cream of tartar, and salt at high speed just until foamy. Gradually add ¾ cup sugar, 2 tablespoons at a time, beating until stiff peaks form and sugar dissolves (2 to 4 minutes).
   Sprinkle one-fourth of flour mixture over beaten egg whites; gently fold in, using a rubber spatula. Repeat procedure with remaining flour mixture, adding one-fourth of mixture at a time. Divide egg white mixture in half.
   Fold vanilla into half of egg white mixture. Gently fold beaten egg yolk mixture into remaining egg white mixture.
   Drop batters alternately by spoonfuls into an ungreased 10-inch tube pan. Gently swirl batters with a knife to create a marbled effect.
   Bake at 350° for 45 to 50 minutes or until cake springs back when lightly touched. Invert pan, and cool 40 minutes. Loosen cake from sides of pan using a narrow metal spatula; remove from pan. Place on a serving plate.
   Drizzle cake with Lemon Glaze. Garnish, if desired. **Yield: one 10-inch cake.**

Lemon Glaze

1½ cups sifted powdered sugar
1 teaspoon grated lemon rind
⅛ teaspoon lemon extract
2 to 3 tablespoons lemon juice

   Combine all ingredients in a small bowl, stirring until smooth. **Yield: about ½ cup.**

Orange Chiffon Cake

2¼ cups sifted cake flour
1 tablespoon baking powder
½ teaspoon salt
1½ cups sugar
½ cup vegetable oil
5 egg yolks
2 teaspoons grated orange rind
¾ cup orange juice
1 teaspoon vanilla extract
8 egg whites
½ teaspoon cream of tartar

   Combine first 4 ingredients in a mixing bowl; make a well in center. Add oil and next 4 ingredients; beat at medium speed of an electric mixer until smooth.
   Beat egg whites and cream of tartar in a large mixing bowl at high speed until soft peaks form. Pour egg yolk mixture in a thin, steady stream over egg whites; gently fold yolks into whites. Pour batter into an ungreased 10-inch tube pan, spreading evenly.
   Bake at 325° for 1 hour or until cake springs back when lightly touched. Invert pan; cool 40 minutes. Loosen cake from sides of pan using a narrow metal spatula; remove from pan. **Yield: one 10-inch cake.**

Peanut Butter Surprise Cake

Peanut Butter Surprise Cake

10 (6-ounce) peanut butter cup candies
1 cup creamy peanut butter
¾ cup butter or margarine, softened
1 cup sugar
¾ cup firmly packed brown sugar
3 large eggs
2 cups all-purpose flour
2 teaspoons baking powder
½ teaspoon salt
1 cup milk
Chocolate-Peanut Butter Frosting
¼ cup chopped roasted peanuts

Freeze peanut butter cup candies. Beat peanut butter and butter at medium speed of an electric mixer until creamy.

Add sugars, beating until light and fluffy. Add eggs, one at a time, beating until blended after each addition.

Combine flour, baking powder, and salt; add to butter mixture alternately with milk, beginning and ending with flour mixture. Beat at low speed until blended after each addition. Coarsely chop frozen candies, and fold into batter.

Pour batter into a greased and floured 13- x 9- x 2-inch pan.

Bake at 350° for 55 minutes to 1 hour or until a wooden pick inserted in center comes out clean. Cool in pan on a wire rack. (Cake may sink slightly in center.)

Spread Chocolate-Peanut Butter Frosting over top of cake. Sprinkle with peanuts. **Yield: 15 servings.**

Chocolate-Peanut Butter Frosting

1 (6-ounce) package semisweet chocolate
    morsels
1⅓ cups creamy peanut butter
½ cup butter or margarine, softened
½ cup sifted powdered sugar

Melt chocolate morsels in a small saucepan over low heat; set aside.

Combine peanut butter, butter, and powdered sugar in a mixing bowl; beat at medium speed of an electric mixer until smooth. Add melted chocolate; beat until smooth. Chill 30 minutes or until spreading consistency. **Yield: 2½ cups.**

Old-Fashioned Gingerbread

½ cup butter or margarine, softened
½ cup sugar
1 large egg
1 cup molasses
2½ cups all-purpose flour
1½ teaspoons baking soda
½ teaspoon salt
1 teaspoon ground cinnamon
1 teaspoon ground cloves
1 teaspoon ground ginger
1 cup hot water
Sweetened whipped cream

Beat butter at medium speed of an electric mixer until creamy; gradually add sugar, beating well. Add egg and molasses, mixing well.

Combine flour and next 5 ingredients; add to butter mixture alternately with water, beginning and ending with flour mixture. Beat at low speed until blended after each addition.

Pour batter into a lightly greased and floured 9-inch square pan.

Bake at 350° for 35 to 40 minutes or until a wooden pick inserted in center comes out clean. Serve with a dollop of whipped cream. **Yield: 9 servings.**

Quick Chocolate-Cola Cake

1 (18.25-ounce) package devil's food cake mix
    without pudding
1 (3.9-ounce) package chocolate instant
    pudding mix
4 large eggs
½ cup vegetable oil
1 (10-ounce) bottle cola-flavored carbonated
    beverage (1¼ cups)
Chocolate-Cola Frosting

Combine first 4 ingredients in a large mixing bowl; beat at low speed of an electric mixer until blended, and set aside.

Bring cola to a boil in a small saucepan over medium heat. With mixer on low speed, gradually pour hot cola into cake batter. Increase speed to medium; beat 2 minutes.

Pour batter into a greased and floured 13- x 9- x 2-inch pan.

Bake at 350° for 30 minutes or until a wooden pick inserted in center comes out clean. Cool in pan on a wire rack 10 minutes.

Spread Chocolate-Cola Frosting over top of warm cake; cool cake completely on wire rack. **Yield: 15 servings.**

Chocolate-Cola Frosting

½ cup butter or margarine
¼ cup plus 2 tablespoons cola-flavored
    carbonated beverage
3 tablespoons cocoa
1 (16-ounce) package powdered sugar, sifted
1 teaspoon vanilla extract
1 cup chopped pecans

Combine first 3 ingredients in a large saucepan; cook over medium heat, stirring constantly, until butter melts. (Do not boil.)

Remove from heat; add powdered sugar and vanilla, stirring until smooth. Stir in pecans. **Yield: about 2¼ cups.**

Pineapple Upside-Down Cake

½ cup butter or margarine
1 cup firmly packed brown sugar
3 (8¼-ounce) cans pineapple slices, undrained
10 pecan halves
11 maraschino cherries, halved
2 large eggs, separated
1 egg yolk
1 cup sugar
1 cup all-purpose flour
1 teaspoon baking powder
½ teaspoon ground cinnamon
¼ teaspoon salt
1 teaspoon vanilla extract
¼ teaspoon cream of tartar

Melt butter in a 10-inch cast-iron skillet over low heat. Sprinkle brown sugar in skillet. Remove from heat.

Drain pineapple, reserving ¼ cup juice. Cut pineapple slices in half, reserving 1 whole slice.

Place whole pineapple slice in center of skillet. Arrange 10 pineapple pieces in a spoke fashion around whole slice in center of skillet.

Place a pecan half and a cherry half between each piece of pineapple. Place a cherry half in center of whole pineapple slice. Arrange remaining pineapple pieces, cut side up, around sides of skillet. Place a cherry half in center of each piece of pineapple around sides of skillet.

Beat 3 egg yolks at medium speed of an electric mixer until thick and pale; gradually add 1 cup sugar, beating well.

Combine flour and next 3 ingredients; stir well. Add to yolk mixture alternately with reserved pineapple juice. Stir in vanilla.

Beat egg whites and cream of tartar at high speed until stiff peaks form; fold into batter. Spoon batter evenly over pineapple in skillet.

Bake at 350° for 45 to 50 minutes or until set. Invert onto a serving plate immediately. Cut into wedges to serve. **Yield: one 10-inch cake.**

Pineapple Upside-Down Cake

Strawberry Shortcake

1 quart strawberries, sliced
¼ to ½ cup sugar
½ cup butter or margarine, softened and divided
2 cups all-purpose flour
1 tablespoon plus 1 teaspoon baking powder
¼ teaspoon salt
¼ cup sugar
Dash of ground nutmeg
½ cup milk
2 large eggs, separated
¼ cup sugar
1 cup whipping cream
¼ cup sifted powdered sugar
Whole strawberries

Combine sliced strawberries and ¼ to ½ cup sugar; stir gently. Cover and chill 1 to 2 hours. Drain.

Butter two 9-inch round cakepans each with ½ tablespoon butter; set aside.

Combine flour and next 4 ingredients in a large mixing bowl; cut in remaining butter with a pastry blender until mixture is crumbly.

Combine milk and egg yolks; beat well. Add to flour mixture; stir with a fork until a soft dough forms. Pat dough out evenly into cakepans. (Dough will be sticky; moisten fingers with water as necessary.)

Beat egg whites at high speed of an electric mixer until stiff but not dry. Gently brush surface of dough with beaten egg whites; sprinkle evenly with ¼ cup sugar.

Bake at 450° for 8 to 10 minutes or until layers are golden. Remove from pans, and cool completely on wire racks. (Layers will be thin.)

Beat whipping cream until foamy; gradually add powdered sugar, beating until soft peaks form.

Place 1 cake layer on a serving plate. Spread half of whipped cream over layer, and arrange half of sliced strawberries on top.

Repeat procedure with remaining layer, whipped cream, and strawberries, reserving a small amount of whipped cream. Garnish cake with remaining whipped cream and whole strawberries. **Yield: one 2-layer cake.**

Orange-Strawberry Shortcake

2 pints fresh strawberries, sliced
2 (11-ounce) cans mandarin oranges, drained
½ cup sugar
1½ tablespoons Triple Sec or other orange-flavored liqueur
2 cups biscuit mix
⅔ cup milk
1 tablespoon sugar
1½ teaspoons ground cinnamon
2 cups whipping cream
½ cup sifted powdered sugar
¼ cup sour cream

Combine first 4 ingredients, stirring until sugar dissolves. Cover and chill 2 hours.

Combine biscuit mix and next 3 ingredients; stir with a fork until dry ingredients are moistened. Turn out onto a floured surface; knead 4 or 5 times. Place dough on a lightly greased baking sheet; press into a 7- x ¾-inch round.

Bake at 425° for 15 minutes or until done. Carefully remove from pan; cool on a wire rack.

Beat whipping cream at medium speed of an electric mixer until foamy; gradually add powdered sugar, beating until soft peaks form. Add sour cream, and beat until firm peaks form.

Split biscuit round in half horizontally. Place bottom half on a serving plate.

Drain fruit, reserving 2 tablespoons liquid. Spoon two-thirds of fruit on bottom round; drizzle with reserved liquid. Spoon half of whipped cream mixture over fruit. Add top biscuit round. Top with remaining fruit and whipped cream. **Yield: 8 servings.**

Orange-Strawberry Shortcake

Chocolate-Raspberry Shortcake

Chocolate-Raspberry Shortcake

½ cup butter or margarine, softened
1¼ cups sugar
2 large eggs, separated
1¼ cups sifted cake flour
2 teaspoons baking powder
¼ teaspoon salt
⅓ cup cocoa
⅔ cup milk
1 teaspoon vanilla extract
2 tablespoons seedless raspberry jam
2 tablespoons Chambord or other raspberry-
    flavored liqueur
2 cups whipping cream
¼ cup sifted powdered sugar
3 cups fresh raspberries
Garnish: fresh mint sprigs

Grease two 9-inch round cakepans; line with wax paper, and grease wax paper. Set aside.

Beat butter at medium speed of an electric mixer 2 minutes or until creamy; gradually add sugar, beating well. Add egg yolks, one at a time, beating until blended after each addition.

Combine flour and next 3 ingredients; add to butter mixture alternately with milk, beginning and ending with flour mixture. Beat at low speed until blended after each addition. Stir in vanilla.

Beat egg whites at high speed until stiff peaks form; fold into batter. Pour batter into pans.

Bake at 350° for 18 minutes or until a wooden pick inserted in center comes out clean. Cool in pans on wire racks 10 minutes. Remove from pans; cool completely on wire racks.

Cook jam in a small saucepan over low heat until melted; stir in liqueur. Set jam mixture aside.

Beat whipping cream at medium speed until foamy; gradually add powdered sugar, beating until soft peaks form.

Place one cake layer on a serving plate; brush with half of jam mixture. Arrange half of raspberries over jam. Spread half of whipped cream over raspberries.

Top with second cake layer; brush with remaining jam mixture. Spread remaining whipped cream over jam mixture; arrange remaining raspberries on top. Garnish, if desired. **Yield: one 9-inch shortcake.**

Pumpkin Roll

(pictured on page 99)

3 large eggs
1 cup sugar
⅔ cup mashed, cooked pumpkin
1 teaspoon lemon juice
¾ cup all-purpose flour
1 teaspoon baking powder
¼ teaspoon salt
1 teaspoon ground cinnamon
1 teaspoon pumpkin pie spice
¼ teaspoon ground nutmeg
1 cup chopped pecans
1 to 2 tablespoons powdered sugar
1 (8-ounce) package cream cheese, softened
⅓ cup butter or margarine, softened
1 cup sifted powdered sugar
1 teaspoon vanilla extract
Garnishes: sweetened whipped cream,
    chopped pecans

Grease and flour a 15- x 10- x 1-inch jellyroll pan; set aside.

Beat eggs in a large bowl at high speed of an electric mixer until thick; gradually add sugar, and beat 5 additional minutes. Stir in pumpkin and lemon juice.

Combine flour and next 5 ingredients; gradually stir into pumpkin mixture. Spread batter evenly in prepared pan; sprinkle with 1 cup pecans, gently pressing into batter.

Bake at 375° for 12 to 15 minutes.

Sift 1 to 2 tablespoons powdered sugar in a 15-x 10-inch rectangle on a cloth towel. When cake is done, immediately loosen from sides of pan, and turn cake out onto sugared towel. Starting at narrow end, roll up cake and towel together; cool on a wire rack, seam side down.

Beat cream cheese and butter at high speed; gradually add 1 cup powdered sugar and vanilla, beating until blended.

Unroll cake; spread with cream cheese mixture, and carefully reroll. Place cake on a serving plate, seam side down. Garnish, if desired. **Yield: 10 servings.**

Roll Up a Perfect Roulage

Don't let the fancy name roulage fool you. This classic rolled cake has its beginning in a jellyroll pan.
• Prepare jellyroll pan according to recipe directions.
• Avoid overbaking; check oven at the lower range of baking time.
• When cake is done, immediately loosen from sides of pan and turn out onto a cloth towel dusted with powdered sugar or cocoa.
• While cake is warm, roll up cake and towel together, beginning at narrow end. Cool cake on a wire rack, seam side down.
• Gently unroll cooled cake, and spread with filling.
• Reroll cake without towel; place on serving plate, seam side down.

Mint-Chocolate Roulage
(pictured on cover)

Vegetable cooking spray
4 large eggs
½ cup water
1 (18.25- or 18.5-ounce) package Swiss
    chocolate, devil's food, or fudge cake mix
2 to 4 tablespoons cocoa
2 cups whipping cream
5 to 6 tablespoons green crème de menthe,
    divided
Cocoa
Chocolate Sauce
Garnish: fresh mint sprigs

Coat two 15- x 10- x 1-inch jellyroll pans with cooking spray; line with wax paper, and coat with cooking spray. Set aside.

Beat eggs in a large mixing bowl at medium-high speed of an electric mixer 5 minutes. Add water, beating at low speed to blend.

Add cake mix gradually, beating at low speed until moistened. Beat at medium-high speed 2 minutes. Divide batter in half, and spread batter evenly into prepared pans. (Layers will be thin.)

Bake each cake at 350° on the middle rack in separate ovens for 13 minutes or until cake springs back when lightly touched in center. (If you don't have a double oven, set 1 pan aside.)

Sift 1 to 2 tablespoons cocoa in a 15- x 10-inch rectangle on a cloth towel; repeat with second towel. When cakes are done, immediately loosen from sides of pans, and turn each out onto a prepared towel.

Peel off wax paper. Starting at narrow end, roll up each cake and towel together; place cakes, seam side down, on wire racks. Cool cakes completely.

Beat whipping cream at medium speed until soft peaks form. Fold in 2 to 3 tablespoons crème de menthe; set aside.

Unroll cake rolls; brush each lightly with 1½ tablespoons crème de menthe. Spread each cake with half of whipped cream mixture. Reroll cakes without towels; place, seam side down, on a baking sheet. Cover and freeze at least 1 hour or up to 3 months.

Dust cakes with cocoa, and drizzle with 2 tablespoons Chocolate Sauce; garnish, if desired. Cut cakes into slices, and serve with remaining Chocolate Sauce. **Yield: 2 filled cake rolls (8 servings each).**

Chocolate Sauce
¾ cup half-and-half
1½ cups semisweet chocolate morsels
1½ cups miniature marshmallows
¼ teaspoon salt
1 teaspoon vanilla extract

Heat half-and-half in a heavy saucepan over low heat. Stir in chocolate morsels, marshmallows, and salt; cook over low heat, stirring constantly, until chocolate and marshmallows melt. Remove from heat, and stir in vanilla. **Yield: 1½ cups.**

Note: You may substitute 1½ teaspoons mint extract and 5 drops of green food coloring for green crème de menthe. Omit brushing cake rolls.

Mint-Chocolate Roulage Technique

While cakes are warm, roll up each cake and towel together, beginning at narrow end.

Cheesecakes & Tortes

These lavish desserts taste as good as they look. And the good news is that all of them in this collection are simple to make and most can be made ahead of time.

Chocolate Praline Torte, Lemon Cheesecake, Apricot Praline Torte

Amaretto-Irish Cream Cheesecake, Chocolate-Glazed Triple Layer Cheesecake

Boston Cream Pie, Chocolate-Mint Baked Alaska Cheesecake, Mocha-Pecan Torte

Lemon Meringue Cream Cups, Blueberries 'n' Cream Cheesecake

Rich White Chocolate Cheesecake (page 50)

From left: Creamy Vanilla, Chocolate Marble, Black Forest, Crème de Menthe, and Praline cheesecakes

Creamy Vanilla Cheesecake

5 (8-ounce) packages cream cheese, softened
1½ cups sugar
3 large eggs
2½ teaspoons vanilla extract
Graham Cracker Crust
Garnish: strawberry fans

Beat cream cheese at high speed of an electric mixer until fluffy; gradually add sugar, beating well. Add eggs, one at a time, beating after each addition. Stir in vanilla. Pour into Graham Cracker Crust.

Bake at 350° for 40 minutes; turn oven off, and partially open oven door. Leave cheesecake in oven 30 minutes. Remove from oven, and cool on a wire rack in a draft-free place.

Cover and chill at least 8 hours. Garnish, if desired. **Yield: 10 to 12 servings.**

Variations

Black Forest Cheesecake: Use Graham Cracker Crust or Chocolate Wafer Crust. Prepare basic cheesecake mixture; stir in 6 ounces melted semisweet chocolate. Pour half of chocolate mixture into crust; top with 1 cup canned dark, sweet, pitted cherries, drained and patted dry. Spoon remaining chocolate mixture evenly over cherries. Bake at 350° for 45 minutes. Garnish with whipped cream and additional cherries, if desired.

Brown Sugar and Spice Cheesecake: Use Gingersnap Crust. For cheesecake mixture, substitute brown sugar for white sugar, and add 1 teaspoon ground cinnamon, ½ teaspoon ground cloves, and ½ teaspoon ground nutmeg when sugar is added. Bake at 350° for 45 minutes. Garnish with whipped cream, and sprinkle with nutmeg, if desired.

Chocolate Marble Cheesecake: Use Chocolate Wafer Crust. Prepare basic cheesecake mixture, and divide in half. Stir 6 ounces melted semisweet chocolate into half of cheesecake mixture. Pour half of plain cheesecake mixture into prepared crust; top with half of chocolate mixture. Repeat layers to use all of mixture. Gently swirl batter with a knife to create a marbled effect. Bake at 350° for 40 minutes. Garnish with mint sprigs, if desired.

Crème de Menthe Cheesecake: Use Chocolate Wafer Crust. Stir ¼ cup green crème de menthe into cheesecake mixture when vanilla is added. Bake at 350° for 45 minutes. Garnish with chocolate leaves, if desired.

Praline Cheesecake: Use Graham Cracker Crust. Substitute dark brown sugar for white sugar in cheesecake mixture. Sauté 1 cup chopped pecans in 3 tablespoons melted butter or margarine; drain pecans on paper towel. Fold into cheesecake mixture when vanilla is added. Bake at 350° for 45 minutes. Garnish with toasted pecan halves, if desired.

Graham Cracker Crust

1⅔ cups graham cracker crumbs
⅓ cup butter or margarine, melted

Combine crumbs and butter; press onto bottom and 1 inch up sides of a 10-inch springform pan. Bake at 350° for 5 minutes. **Yield: one 10-inch crust.**

Variations

Chocolate Wafer Crust: Substitute 1⅔ cups chocolate wafer crumbs for graham cracker crumbs.

Gingersnap Crust: Substitute 1⅔ cups gingersnap crumbs for graham cracker crumbs.

Amaretto-Irish Cream Cheesecake

1½ cups vanilla wafer crumbs
½ cup blanched whole almonds, toasted and finely chopped
¼ cup butter or margarine, melted
1 tablespoon amaretto
3 (8-ounce) packages cream cheese, softened
1 cup sugar
4 large eggs
⅓ cup whipping cream
⅓ cup blanched whole almonds, toasted and ground
¼ cup Irish Cream liqueur
¼ cup amaretto
1½ cups sour cream
1 tablespoon sugar
½ teaspoon vanilla extract
¼ cup sliced almonds

Combine first 4 ingredients; press onto bottom of a lightly greased 10-inch springform pan.

Bake at 350° for 10 minutes. Cool.

Beat cream cheese at high speed of an electric mixer until fluffy; gradually add 1 cup sugar, beating well. Add eggs, one at a time, beating after each addition. Stir in whipping cream and next 3 ingredients; pour into prepared crust.

Bake at 350° for 50 minutes; turn oven off, and leave cheesecake in oven 30 minutes.

Combine sour cream and next 2 ingredients; stir and spoon over cheesecake. Sprinkle ¼ cup sliced almonds around edge.

Bake at 500° for 5 minutes. Cool; cover and chill at least 8 hours. **Yield: 10 to 12 servings.**

Blueberries 'n' Cream Cheesecake

2½ cups fresh blueberries
1 tablespoon cornstarch
3 (8-ounce) packages cream cheese, softened
1 cup sugar
5 large eggs
2 tablespoons cornstarch
¼ teaspoon salt
1½ cups sour cream
2 tablespoons sugar
½ teaspoon vanilla extract
¼ cup sugar
¼ cup water
1 cup fresh blueberries

Combine 2½ cups blueberries and 1 tablespoon cornstarch in container of an electric blender; cover and process until smooth. Cook puree in saucepan over medium-high heat about 15 minutes or until slightly thickened, stirring constantly. Set aside to cool. Reserve ½ cup puree for glaze.

Beat cream cheese at medium speed of an electric mixer until fluffy. Gradually add 1 cup sugar, mixing well. Add eggs, one at a time, beating after each addition. Stir in 2 tablespoons cornstarch and salt.

Pour batter into a greased 9-inch springform pan. Pour puree over cheesecake batter; gently swirl with a knife.

Bake at 325° for 45 minutes or until set. Remove from oven; cool on a wire rack 20 minutes.

Combine sour cream, 2 tablespoons sugar, and vanilla in a small bowl; spread over cheesecake.

Bake at 325° for 10 additional minutes. Cool on wire rack. Cover and chill 8 hours.

Combine reserved ½ cup puree, ¼ cup sugar, and water in a small saucepan; cook over medium heat, stirring constantly, until thickened. Gently fold in 1 cup blueberries; cool.

Remove sides of springform pan, and spoon blueberry glaze on cheesecake. **Yield: 10 to 12 servings.**

Chocolate-Glazed Triple Layer Cheesecake

1 (9-ounce) package chocolate wafer cookies, crushed (about 2 cups)
¾ cup sugar, divided
¼ cup plus 1 tablespoon butter or margarine, melted
2 (8-ounce) packages cream cheese, softened and divided
3 large eggs, divided
¼ teaspoon vanilla extract
2 (1-ounce) squares semisweet chocolate, melted
1⅓ cups sour cream, divided
⅓ cup firmly packed dark brown sugar
1 tablespoon all-purpose flour
½ teaspoon vanilla extract
¼ cup chopped pecans
5 ounces cream cheese, softened
¼ teaspoon vanilla extract
¼ teaspoon almond extract
Chocolate Glaze
Garnish: chocolate leaves

Combine cookie crumbs, ¼ cup sugar, and butter; press onto bottom and 2 inches up sides of a 9-inch springform pan. Set aside.

Beat 1 (8-ounce) package cream cheese at medium speed of an electric mixer until fluffy; gradually add ¼ cup sugar, beating well. Add 1 egg and ¼ teaspoon vanilla; mix well. Stir in melted chocolate and ⅓ cup sour cream. Spoon over prepared crust.

Beat remaining 1 (8-ounce) package cream cheese until fluffy; gradually add brown sugar and flour, beating well. Add 1 egg and ½ teaspoon vanilla; mix well. Stir in pecans. Spoon gently over chocolate layer.

Beat 5 ounces cream cheese and remaining ¼ cup sugar until fluffy. Add 1 egg; mix well. Stir in remaining 1 cup sour cream, ¼ teaspoon vanilla, and almond extract. Spoon gently over praline layer.

Chocolate-Glazed Triple Layer Cheesecake

Bake at 325° for 1 hour. Turn oven off; leave cheesecake in oven, with oven door closed, 30 minutes. Partially open door; leave cheesecake in oven 30 additional minutes. Cool. Cover and chill 8 hours. Remove sides of springform pan.

Spread Chocolate Glaze over cheesecake. Garnish, if desired. **Yield: 10 to 12 servings.**

Chocolate Glaze

6 (1-ounce) squares semisweet chocolate
¼ cup butter or margarine
¾ cup sifted powdered sugar
2 tablespoons water
1 teaspoon vanilla extract

Melt chocolate and butter in a heavy saucepan over low heat, stirring occasionally. Remove from heat; stir in sugar, water, and vanilla.

Spread over cheesecake while glaze is warm. **Yield: enough for one 9-inch cheesecake.**

Rich White Chocolate Cheesecake

(pictured on page 45)

2 cups chocolate wafer crumbs
2 tablespoons sugar
¼ cup plus 2 tablespoons butter or
    margarine, melted
4 (8-ounce) packages cream cheese, softened
1 cup sugar
4 large eggs
½ cup Irish Cream liqueur
1 tablespoon vanilla extract
½ pound premium white chocolate, chopped
Garnish: marbled chocolate curls

Combine first 3 ingredients in a medium bowl; press onto bottom and 2 inches up sides of a 10-inch springform pan. Bake at 325° for 6 to 8 minutes. Set aside, and cool.

Beat cream cheese at medium speed of an electric mixer until fluffy; gradually add 1 cup sugar, beating well. Add eggs, one at a time, beating after each addition. Stir in liqueur and vanilla. Add chopped white chocolate; stir. Pour into crust.

Bake at 325° for 50 to 60 minutes or until set. Turn oven off, and partially open oven door; leave cheesecake in oven 1 hour. Remove cheesecake from oven, and cool in pan on a wire rack. Cover and chill thoroughly.

Remove sides of springform pan. Garnish, if desired. **Yield: 10 to 12 servings.**

Note: To make marbled chocolate curls, pour 12 ounces melted semisweet chocolate onto a smooth surface, such as marble or an aluminum foil-lined cookie sheet. Pour 12 ounces melted white chocolate over semisweet chocolate layer. Using a small spatula, swirl chocolates to create a marbled effect, covering about a 12- x 9-inch area. Let stand at room temperature until chocolate feels slightly tacky but not firm. (If chocolate is too hard, curls will break; if too soft, chocolate will not curl.) Pull a cheese plane across chocolate to form curls.

Chocolate-Mint Baked Alaska Cheesecake

1 cup chocolate wafer crumbs
2 tablespoons sugar
3 tablespoons butter or margarine, melted
1 cup mint chocolate morsels
3 (8-ounce) packages cream cheese, softened
⅔ cup sugar
3 large eggs
1 teaspoon vanilla extract
3 egg whites
1 (7-ounce) jar marshmallow cream

Combine first 3 ingredients; press onto bottom of a 9-inch springform pan.

Bake at 350° for 10 minutes; set aside.

Melt chocolate morsels in a small heavy saucepan over low heat, stirring constantly. Set mixture aside.

Beat cream cheese at medium speed of an electric mixer until fluffy; gradually add ⅔ cup sugar, beating well. Add eggs, one at a time, beating after each addition. Stir in melted chocolate and vanilla. Pour into prepared crust.

Bake at 350° for 50 minutes.

Remove from oven; immediately run a knife around sides of cheesecake to loosen, and cool completely in pan on a wire rack. Cover and chill 8 hours.

Beat egg whites at high speed of an electric mixer until soft peaks form. Gradually add marshmallow cream, beating until stiff peaks form. Remove sides of springform pan. Carefully spread egg white mixture over top and sides of cake.

Bake at 325° for 25 to 30 minutes or until golden. Serve immediately. **Yield: 10 to 12 servings.**

Lemon Cheesecake

¾ cup graham cracker crumbs
2 tablespoons sugar
1 tablespoon ground cinnamon
1 tablespoon butter or margarine, softened
5 (8-ounce) packages cream cheese, softened
1⅔ cups sugar
5 large eggs
⅛ teaspoon salt
1½ teaspoons vanilla extract
¼ cup lemon juice

Combine first 3 ingredients; stir well, and set aside. Grease bottom and sides of a 10-inch springform pan with butter. Add crumb mixture; tilt pan to coat sides and bottom. Chill.

Beat cream cheese at medium speed of an electric mixer until fluffy; gradually add 1⅔ cups sugar, beating well. Add eggs, one at a time, beating after each addition. Stir in salt, vanilla, and lemon juice; pour into prepared crust.

Bake at 300° for 1 hour and 20 minutes. (Center may be soft but will set when chilled.) Cool on a wire rack; cover and chill 8 hours. **Yield: 10 to 12 servings.**

Sour Cream-Almond Dessert

¾ cup butter or margarine, softened
1½ cups all-purpose flour
½ cup chopped almonds
2 tablespoons sugar
¾ to 1 cup almond paste, broken into small
    pieces
4 large eggs
1 cup sugar
2 tablespoons cornstarch
1 (16-ounce) carton sour cream
1 pint whipping cream
3 tablespoons powdered sugar
¼ cup sliced almonds, toasted

Combine first 4 ingredients in a large mixing bowl; beat at medium speed of an electric mixer until blended. Spread mixture onto bottom and 1½ inches up sides of an ungreased 9-inch springform pan.

Bake at 400° for 10 minutes or until lightly browned; set aside.

Combine almond paste, eggs, and 1 cup sugar; beat at medium speed of an electric mixer until blended (about 4 minutes). Combine cornstarch and sour cream; stir into almond paste mixture, and pour into prepared crust.

Bake at 325° for 1 hour or until lightly browned (center will be a little soft). Cool on a wire rack; cover and chill at least 8 hours.

Remove sides of springform pan. Beat whipping cream until foamy; gradually add powdered sugar, beating until soft peaks form. Set aside 1 cup whipped cream, and spread remaining whipped cream on top of dessert. Pipe or dollop reserved whipped cream around outer edges, and sprinkle with toasted almonds. **Yield: 8 to 10 servings.**

Sour Cream-Almond Dessert

Boston Cream Pie

Boston Cream Pie

½ cup butter or margarine, softened
1 cup sugar
3 large eggs
2 cups sifted cake flour
2 teaspoons baking powder
¼ teaspoon salt
½ cup milk
2 teaspoons vanilla extract
Cream Filling
Chocolate Glaze

Beat butter at medium speed of an electric mixer until creamy; gradually add sugar, beating well. Add eggs, one at a time, beating after each addition.

Combine flour, baking powder, and salt; add to butter mixture alternately with milk, beginning and ending with flour mixture. Mix after each addition. Stir in vanilla.

Pour batter into 2 greased and floured 9-inch round cakepans.

Bake at 350° for 20 to 25 minutes or until a wooden pick inserted in center comes out clean. Cool in pans on wire racks 10 minutes; remove from pans, and cool completely on wire racks.

Spread Cream Filling between cake layers. Spread Chocolate Glaze over top of cake, letting excess drip down sides of cake. Chill until ready to serve. **Yield: 8 to 10 servings.**

Cream Filling

½ cup sugar
¼ cup cornstarch
¼ teaspoon salt
2 cups milk
4 egg yolks, lightly beaten
1 teaspoon vanilla extract

Combine first 3 ingredients in a heavy saucepan. Add milk and egg yolks, stirring with a wire whisk until blended.

Cook over medium heat, stirring constantly, until mixture comes to a boil. Boil 1 minute or until thickened, stirring constantly; remove from heat. Stir in vanilla; cool. **Yield: 2½ cups.**

Chocolate Glaze

2 tablespoons butter or margarine
1 (1-ounce) square unsweetened chocolate
1 cup sifted powdered sugar
2 tablespoons boiling water

Melt butter and chocolate in a saucepan, stirring constantly. Cool slightly. Add powdered sugar and water; beat until smooth. **Yield: ½ cup.**

Chocolate Praline Torte

1½ cups chopped walnuts
1½ cups vanilla wafer crumbs
1 cup firmly packed brown sugar
1 cup butter or margarine, melted
1 (18.5-ounce) package devil's food cake mix without pudding
1½ cups whipping cream
3 tablespoons sifted powdered sugar
1 teaspoon vanilla extract

Combine first 4 ingredients. Sprinkle about ¾ cup of walnut mixture in each of 4 ungreased 9-inch round cakepans, pressing lightly into pans.

Prepare cake mix according to package directions; pour over walnut mixture in pans.

Bake at 350° for 15 to 20 minutes or until a wooden pick inserted in center comes out clean. Remove from pans, and cool on wire racks.

Beat whipping cream at medium speed of an electric mixer until foamy; gradually add powdered sugar, beating until firm peaks form. Stir in vanilla.

Place 1 layer, nut side up, on a serving plate. Spread ¾ cup whipped cream over layer. Repeat with remaining 3 layers, ending with whipped cream; chill. **Yield: one 9-inch torte.**

Apricot Praline Torte

1 (16-ounce) loaf pound cake
1 cup apricot preserves
Praline Buttercream
Sifted powdered sugar

Cut pound cake loaf horizontally into 3 layers.

Melt apricot preserves in a small saucepan over low heat. Spread half of preserves over bottom layer of cake. Spread half of Praline Buttercream over preserves, and place second layer of cake on buttercream.

Repeat procedure with remaining preserves and buttercream; top with remaining layer of cake. Sprinkle cake lightly with sifted powdered sugar. **Yield: 10 to 12 servings.**

Praline Buttercream

½ cup unsalted butter, softened
2½ cups sifted powdered sugar
2 to 3 tablespoons whipping cream
½ cup Praline Powder
1 teaspoon vanilla extract

Beat butter at medium speed of an electric mixer until creamy; gradually add sugar, beating well. Beat in whipping cream; fold in Praline Powder and vanilla. **Yield: 2 cups.**

Praline Powder

2 tablespoons butter
¼ cup sugar
¾ cup almonds, chopped and toasted

Cook butter and sugar in a saucepan over medium heat until sugar melts and turns a light caramel color (mixture will separate), stirring occasionally. Remove from heat; stir in almonds.

Pour onto a greased aluminum foil-lined baking sheet; cool. Break into chunks. Position knife blade in food processor bowl; add chunks of praline. Process until finely crushed. **Yield: 1 cup.**

Toffee Meringue Torte

6 egg whites
¾ teaspoon cream of tartar
1 cup superfine sugar
8 (1.4-ounce) English toffee-flavored candy
    bars, frozen and crushed
2½ cups whipping cream, whipped
Toffee Sauce

Line 2 baking sheets with parchment paper. Trace a 9-inch circle on each, using a 9-inch cakepan as a guide. Turn paper over; set aside.

Beat egg whites at high speed of an electric mixer until foamy; add cream of tartar, beating until soft peaks form. Add sugar, 2 tablespoons at a time, beating until stiff peaks form. Spoon meringue mixture evenly inside circles on baking sheets. Form each into a smooth circle.

Bake at 275° for 2 hours. Turn oven off; cool slightly. Remove from oven; peel off paper. Dry meringues on wire racks, away from drafts.

Reserve 2 tablespoons crushed candy for garnish. Fold remaining crushed candy into whipped cream. Chill or freeze until firm, but spreadable.

Spread whipped cream mixture between layers of meringue and on top and sides. Garnish with reserved candy. Place torte in an airtight cake cover; freeze at least 8 hours. Cut into wedges; serve with Toffee Sauce. **Yield: 8 to 10 servings.**

Toffee Sauce

1½ cups firmly packed brown sugar
½ cup light corn syrup
⅓ cup butter
⅔ cup whipping cream
1 teaspoon butter flavoring

Combine first 3 ingredients in a saucepan. Cook over medium heat until mixture comes to a full boil, stirring frequently. Remove from heat; cool 5 minutes. Stir in whipping cream and flavoring. Serve warm with torte. **Yield: 2 cups.**

Toffee Meringue Torte

Mocha-Pecan Torte

Mocha-Pecan Torte

8 eggs, separated
⅔ cup sifted powdered sugar
1 teaspoon baking powder
⅓ cup cocoa
⅓ cup soft breadcrumbs
1 teaspoon vanilla extract
2 cups ground pecans
Mocha Buttercream Frosting
Chocolate candy sprinkles

Line the bottom of 4 (8-inch) round cakepans with wax paper. Grease and flour paper; set aside.

Combine egg yolks, sugar, and baking powder; beat at high speed of an electric mixer 2 to 3 minutes or until mixture is thick and pale.

Combine cocoa and breadcrumbs; stir into egg yolk mixture. Stir in vanilla; fold in pecans.

Beat egg whites in a mixing bowl until stiff peaks form; fold one-fourth of egg whites into yolk mixture. Fold remaining egg whites into yolk mixture. Pour into pans; spread tops to smooth.

Bake at 350° for 15 minutes or until layers spring back when lightly touched. Cool in pans on wire racks 5 minutes. Invert layers onto wire racks; peel off wax paper. (Layers will be thin.) Cool.

Set aside 1½ cups frosting. Spread 3 cups frosting between layers and on sides and top of torte. Pat sprinkles onto sides. Score frosting on top of torte into 12 wedges. Spoon reserved frosting into a decorating bag fitted with a No. 2F metal tip. Pipe 12 rosettes around top edge; sprinkle rosettes with sprinkles. Chill. **Yield: one 8-inch torte.**

Mocha Buttercream Frosting

2½ teaspoons instant coffee granules
2 tablespoons water
¾ cup plus 2 tablespoons butter, softened
1 tablespoon plus 2 teaspoons cocoa
7 cups sifted powdered sugar
⅓ cup half-and-half
1 teaspoon vanilla extract

Dissolve coffee granules in water; set aside. Beat butter at medium speed of an electric mixer until creamy. Add coffee mixture and cocoa; beat well. Add sugar alternately with half-and-half; beat until fluffy. Stir in vanilla. **Yield: 4½ cups.**

Lemon Meringue Cream Cups

2 egg whites
Pinch of salt
1 teaspoon lemon juice
½ cup sugar
Lemon Cream Filling
Garnishes: whipped cream, grated lemon rind

Beat first 3 ingredients at high speed of an electric mixer until foamy. Add sugar, 1 tablespoon at a time, beating until stiff peaks form. (Do not underbeat.)

Line a baking sheet with parchment paper. Spoon meringue into 6 equal portions on paper. Shape meringue into circles about 3 inches in diameter; shape each circle into a shell (sides should be about 1 to 1½ inches high).

Bake at 275° for 1 hour. Turn oven off; cool in oven several hours.

Peel off paper. Spoon Lemon Cream Filling into shells. Garnish, if desired. **Yield: 6 servings.**

Lemon Cream Filling

3 large eggs
½ cup sugar
3 tablespoons lemon juice
1½ teaspoons grated lemon rind
½ cup whipping cream, whipped

Beat eggs until thick and pale. Add sugar and lemon juice; beat well. Stir in lemon rind.

Cook over low heat, stirring constantly, until mixture thickens and reaches 160°. Cool thoroughly. Fold whipped cream into cooled mixture. **Yield: about 1½ cups.**

Coffee Meringues with Butterscotch Mousse

3 egg whites
1 teaspoon instant coffee granules
¼ teaspoon cream of tartar
1 cup sugar
Butterscotch Mousse

Beat first 3 ingredients at high speed of an electric mixer until foamy. Add sugar, 1 tablespoon at a time, beating until stiff peaks form.

Line baking sheets with unglazed brown paper or parchment paper. (Do not use recycled paper.) Spoon meringue by rounded teaspoonfuls onto paper. Make an indentation in center of each with back of a spoon.

Bake at 225° for 1 hour and 15 minutes; turn oven off, and cool in oven 2 hours or overnight.

Remove meringues from paper; store in an airtight container up to 1 week. Just before serving, spoon Butterscotch Mousse into each meringue. **Yield: 4½ dozen.**

Butterscotch Mousse

1 cup butterscotch morsels
3 tablespoons butter or margarine
1 tablespoon instant coffee granules
3 tablespoons water
1 large egg, lightly beaten
1 cup whipping cream, whipped

Combine first 4 ingredients in a heavy saucepan; cook over low heat, stirring constantly, until morsels and butter melt.

Stir about one-fourth of hot mixture into egg; add to remaining hot mixture, stirring constantly. Cook over medium heat, stirring constantly, 1 minute. Remove from heat, and cool to room temperature.

Fold in whipped cream. Cover and chill 8 hours. **Yield: 2⅔ cups.**

Pavlova

1 teaspoon cornstarch
4 egg whites
1 cup sugar
1 teaspoon white vinegar
1 teaspoon vanilla extract
1½ cups whipping cream
2 tablespoons strawberry jam
1 tablespoon water
1 banana
Lemon juice
2 kiwifruit, peeled and sliced
1 pint strawberries, halved
Garnish: strawberry fans

Mark an 11- x 7-inch rectangle on wax paper; place on baking sheet. Grease wax paper, and dust with cornstarch. Set aside.

Beat egg whites at high speed of an electric mixer until foamy. Gradually add sugar, ¼ cup at a time, beating until stiff peaks form (2 to 4 minutes). Beat in vinegar and vanilla. Spread meringue onto rectangle.

Bake at 275° for 45 minutes. Carefully remove meringue from baking sheet, and cool on a wire rack. Carefully turn meringue over, and remove wax paper. Place meringue, right side up, on a platter.

Beat whipping cream at medium speed until soft peaks form. Set aside 1 cup whipped cream.

Spread remaining whipped cream over meringue, leaving a 1-inch border. Pipe or dollop reserved whipped cream around edges.

Combine jam and water in a small saucepan; heat just until jam melts, stirring constantly. Pour mixture through a wire-mesh strainer into a bowl, discarding seeds; set liquid aside to cool.

Slice banana, and sprinkle with lemon juice. Arrange banana, kiwifruit, and strawberry halves on whipped cream. Brush strawberries with strawberry liquid. Garnish, if desired. Serve immediately. **Yield: 10 to 12 servings.**

Frozen Favorites

Don't wait for summer to enjoy these frosty favorites. Use your freezer to churn out ice creams, sherbets, and sorbets any time of year. Or start with commercial ice cream to create a tempting treat.

Strawberries and Cream, Piña Colada Ice Cream, Champagne Ice

Frozen Viennese Torte, Brownie Baked Alaska, Chocolate Ice Cream Brownies

Pineapple-Orange Sherbet, Watermelon Sherbet, Blackberry Sorbet, Praline Freeze

Caramel-Toffee Bombe, Spumoni Charlotte, Frozen Almond Crunch

Fresh Peach Ice Cream (page 63)

Basic Vanilla Ice Cream

2 (14-ounce) cans sweetened condensed milk
1 quart half-and-half
1 tablespoon plus 1 teaspoon vanilla extract

Combine all ingredients, mixing well. Pour mixture into freezer container of a 1-gallon hand-turned or electric freezer.

Freeze according to manufacturer's instructions. Pack freezer with additional ice and rock salt, and let stand 1 hour. **Yield: 2½ quarts.**

Variations

Black Forest Ice Cream: Stir in ½ cup chocolate syrup and 1 (16½-ounce) can pitted Bing cherries, drained and halved, before freezing.

Blueberry Ice Cream: Stir in 2 cups fresh or frozen blueberries before freezing.

Butter Pecan Ice Cream: Stir in 1 tablespoon butter flavoring and 2 cups coarsely chopped toasted pecans before freezing.

Cherry-Pecan Ice Cream: Substitute 1 teaspoon almond extract for vanilla, and add ⅓ cup maraschino cherry juice to ice cream mixture; freeze as directed. Stir in ¾ cup quartered maraschino cherries and ¾ cup chopped pecans.

Chocolate-Covered Peanut Ice Cream: Stir in ½ cup chocolate syrup and 2 (7-ounce) packages chocolate-covered peanuts before freezing.

Coffee Ice Cream: Combine ⅔ cup hot water and 1 tablespoon instant coffee granules, stirring until granules dissolve. Cool slightly. Stir in before freezing.

Cookies and Cream Ice Cream: Break 15 cream-filled chocolate sandwich cookies into small pieces; stir in before freezing.

Double Chocolate Ice Cream: Stir in ½ cup chocolate syrup and 1 (6-ounce) package semisweet chocolate mini-morsels before freezing.

Lemonade Ice Cream: Stir in 1 (6-ounce) can frozen lemonade concentrate, thawed and undiluted, before freezing.

Mint-Chocolate Chip Ice Cream: Stir in ½ cup green crème de menthe and 1 (6-ounce) package semisweet chocolate mini-morsels before freezing.

Mocha Ice Cream: Combine 1 cup hot water and 1 tablespoon instant coffee granules, stirring until granules dissolve. Cool slightly. Stir in coffee mixture and ½ cup chocolate syrup before freezing.

Peanut Butter Ice Cream: Stir in ¾ cup chunky peanut butter before freezing. Serve with chocolate syrup, if desired.

Rainbow Candy Ice Cream: Stir in 1½ cups candy-coated milk chocolate pieces before freezing.

Strawberry-Banana-Nut Ice Cream: Stir in 3 bananas, mashed; 1 pint strawberries, coarsely chopped; and ¾ cup chopped pecans before freezing.

Toffee Ice Cream: Stir in 1 (6-ounce) package toffee-flavored candy pieces before freezing.

Butter Crisp Ice Cream

2 cups finely crushed cornflakes cereal
2 cups chopped pecans
1 cup firmly packed brown sugar
½ cup butter or margarine, melted
4 envelopes unflavored gelatin
2 cups sugar
¼ teaspoon salt
6 cups milk, divided
6 large eggs, lightly beaten
1 quart whipping cream
2 tablespoons vanilla extract

Combine first 3 ingredients; stir in butter. Spoon mixture into a 15- x 10- x 1-inch jellyroll pan. Bake at 350° for 25 minutes, stirring occasionally; cool. Set aside.

Combine gelatin, sugar, and salt in a large saucepan; stir in 2 cups milk. Let stand 1 minute.

Cook over low heat, stirring until gelatin dissolves (about 5 minutes).

Stir a small amount of hot milk mixture gradually into eggs; add to remaining hot milk mixture, stirring constantly. Cook over medium heat, stirring often, until thermometer registers 160° (3 to 5 minutes). Add remaining 4 cups milk, whipping cream, and vanilla.

Pour mixture into freezer container of a 5-quart hand-turned or electric freezer. Freeze according to manufacturer's instructions.

Spoon ice cream into a large airtight container, and stir in reserved cornflakes mixture. Cover and freeze. **Yield: 1 gallon.**

Strawberries and Cream

1 quart milk
1 pint half-and-half
2 (14-ounce) cans sweetened condensed milk
2 teaspoons vanilla extract
⅛ to ¼ teaspoon almond extract
1 quart fresh strawberries, sliced

Combine first 5 ingredients in a large bowl. Pour mixture into freezer container of a 5-quart hand-turned or electric freezer.

Freeze according to manufacturer's instructions. Pack freezer with additional ice and rock salt, and let stand 1 hour before serving. Serve with sliced strawberries. **Yield: 3 quarts.**

From left: Butter Crisp Ice Cream, Peanut Ice Cream (page 65), and Strawberries and Cream

Honey-Vanilla Ice Cream

Honey-Vanilla Ice Cream

2 cups sugar
⅓ cup all-purpose flour
¼ teaspoon salt
4 cups milk
5 large eggs, beaten
5 cups half-and-half
1 tablespoon vanilla extract
½ cup honey

Combine first 3 ingredients; stir well, and set sugar mixture aside.

Heat milk in a heavy 3-quart saucepan over low heat just until hot. Gradually add sugar mixture, stirring until blended. Cook over medium heat, stirring constantly, 10 minutes or until thickened.

Stir about one-fourth of hot milk mixture gradually into beaten eggs; add to remaining hot milk mixture, stirring constantly. Cook 1 minute, stirring constantly. Remove from heat, and cool. Cover and chill at least 2 hours.

Stir half-and-half and vanilla into chilled custard mixture. Pour into freezer container of a 1-gallon hand-turned or electric freezer.

Freeze according to manufacturer's instructions. Remove dasher, and stir in honey. Pack freezer with additional ice and rock salt, and let stand 1 hour before serving. **Yield: 3 quarts.**

Honey-Vanilla Ice Cream Technique

Remove dasher from frozen ice cream, and stir in honey. Let ice cream ripen 1 hour.

Fresh Peach Ice Cream

(pictured on page 59)

1⅓ cups sugar
¼ cup all-purpose flour
¼ teaspoon salt
3⅓ cups milk
3 large eggs, beaten
4 cups peeled, mashed fresh peaches
⅔ cup sugar
1⅔ cups half-and-half
1 cup whipping cream
2 teaspoons vanilla extract
1 teaspoon almond extract
Garnish: toasted sliced almonds

Combine first 3 ingredients; stir well, and set sugar mixture aside.

Heat milk in a heavy 3-quart saucepan over low heat just until hot. Gradually add sugar mixture, stirring until blended. Cook over medium heat, stirring constantly, 10 minutes or until thickened.

Stir about one-fourth of hot milk mixture gradually into beaten eggs; add to remaining hot milk mixture, stirring constantly. Cook 1 minute, stirring constantly. Remove from heat, and cool. Cover and chill at least 2 hours.

Combine mashed peaches and ⅔ cup sugar; stir well, and set aside.

Combine half-and-half and next 3 ingredients in a large bowl; stir well. Add chilled custard mixture, stirring with a wire whisk. Stir in reserved peach mixture. Pour into freezer container of a 1-gallon hand-turned or electric freezer.

Freeze according to manufacturer's instructions. Pack freezer with additional ice and rock salt, and let stand 1½ to 2 hours before serving. Garnish each serving, if desired. **Yield: 3 quarts.**

Piña Colada Ice Cream

6 **large eggs, beaten**
1½ **cups sugar**
5 **cups milk**
2 **cups half-and-half**
1 **cup whipping cream**
1 **(10-ounce) can frozen piña colada tropical**
    fruit mixer, thawed and undiluted
½ **cup light rum**
Garnish: toasted coconut

Combine eggs and sugar in a large heavy saucepan; gradually add milk, beating well. Cook mixture over medium heat, stirring constantly,

until thermometer registers 160°. Remove from heat, and cool.

Stir in half-and-half and next 3 ingredients.

Pour mixture into container of a 1-gallon hand-turned or electric freezer.

Freeze according to manufacturer's instructions. Pack freezer with additional ice and rock salt, and let stand 1 hour before serving (ice cream will be soft). Garnish each serving, if desired. **Yield: about 1 gallon.**

Note: To scoop ice cream into balls as shown in photograph, spoon into an airtight container after standing time. Cover; freeze at least 8 hours.

Piña Colada Ice Cream

Frangelica Cream

⅔ cup hazelnuts or slivered almonds
¾ cup sugar
1¾ cups milk
½ cup sugar, divided
5 egg yolks
¼ cup Frangelica or other hazelnut-flavored
    liqueur
1 cup whipping cream

Place hazelnuts in a shallow pan, and bake at 350° for 15 minutes; cool. Remove loose skins by rubbing nuts together. Chop nuts, and set aside.

Cook ¾ cup sugar in a heavy saucepan over medium heat, stirring occasionally, until caramelized (sugar melts and turns golden). Remove from heat; add nuts, and stir. Immediately pour into a buttered jellyroll pan. Cool 1 hour. Break brittle into small pieces.

Combine milk and 2 tablespoons sugar in a heavy saucepan; cook over medium heat until mixture boils.

Beat egg yolks and remaining 6 tablespoons sugar at medium speed of an electric mixer until thick and pale. Gradually stir about one-fourth of milk mixture into yolks; add to remaining milk mixture, stirring constantly.

Add Frangelica, and cook over low heat 5 minutes or until mixture reaches 160° (it does not thicken). Do not boil. Cover and chill. Add whipping cream and brittle.

Pour mixture into freezer container of a 2-quart hand-turned or electric freezer.

Freeze according to manufacturer's instructions. Pack freezer with additional ice and rock salt, and let stand 1 hour before serving. **Yield: about 1½ quarts.**

Peanut Ice Cream

(pictured on page 61)

6 large eggs, lightly beaten
1 cup firmly packed brown sugar
3 cups milk
⅔ cup creamy peanut butter
3 cups whipping cream
2 cups unsalted peanuts, coarsely chopped
Commercial hot fudge sauce
Garnish: chopped peanuts

Combine eggs and brown sugar; set aside.

Heat milk in a large heavy saucepan over medium heat until hot. Gradually stir a small amount of hot milk into egg mixture; add to remaining hot milk, stirring constantly. Cook over medium heat, stirring often, until thermometer registers 160° (3 to 5 minutes).

Remove from heat; stir in peanut butter, and cool. Stir in whipping cream and peanuts.

Pour mixture into freezer container of a 1-gallon hand-turned or electric freezer.

Freeze according to manufacturer's instructions. Pack freezer with additional ice and rock salt, and let stand 1 hour. Serve with hot fudge sauce. Garnish, if desired. **Yield: 2½ quarts.**

Champagne Ice

1½ cups sugar
3 cups water
1½ tablespoons grated lemon rind
⅓ cup fresh lemon juice
2 (750-milliliter) bottles champagne

Combine all ingredients in freezer container of a 1-gallon hand-turned or electric freezer; stir mixture well.

Freeze according to manufacturer's instructions. Pack freezer with additional ice and rock salt, and let stand 1 hour. **Yield: 2½ quarts.**

Apricot Sherbet

2 (16-ounce) cans apricot halves in light
   syrup, drained
2 cups sugar
1 quart milk
¼ cup lemon juice

Place apricots in container of an electric
blender; cover and process until smooth, stopping
once to scrape down sides.

Combine apricot puree, sugar, milk, and
lemon juice. Pour into freezer container of a 1-
gallon hand-turned or electric freezer.

Freeze according to manufacturer's instructions. Pack freezer with additional ice and rock
salt, and let stand 1 hour. **Yield: 2 quarts.**

Pineapple-Orange Sherbet

1 (8-ounce) can crushed pineapple, undrained
2 (14-ounce) cans sweetened condensed milk
6 (12-ounce) cans orange carbonated beverage

Combine pineapple and condensed milk in
freezer container of a 1-gallon hand-turned or
electric freezer; stir well. Add orange beverage,
stirring well.

Freeze according to manufacturer's instructions. Pack freezer with additional ice and rock
salt, and let stand 1 hour. **Yield: 1 gallon.**

Watermelon Sherbet

4 cups diced and seeded watermelon
¾ to 1 cup sugar
3 tablespoons lemon juice
Dash of salt
1 envelope unflavored gelatin
¼ cup cold water
1 cup whipping cream

Combine first 4 ingredients in a large bowl;
cover and chill 30 minutes.

Spoon mixture into container of an electric
blender; cover and process until smooth. Return
to bowl.

Sprinkle gelatin over cold water in a saucepan; let stand 1 minute. Cook over low heat until
gelatin dissolves; add to watermelon mixture,
stirring well.

Add whipping cream; beat at medium speed
of an electric mixer until fluffy. Pour into freezer
container of a 1-gallon hand-turned or electric
freezer.

Freeze according to manufacturer's instructions. Serve immediately as mixture does not
need ripening. **Yield: 1 quart.**

Blackberry Sorbet

1 cup sugar
1 cup water
2 (16-ounce) packages frozen blackberries,
   thawed and divided
3 large ripe pears, peeled, cored, and chopped
¼ cup plus 2 tablespoons orange juice

Combine sugar and water in a medium saucepan; cook over medium heat until sugar dissolves, stirring constantly. Cool slightly; transfer
to a large bowl. Cover and chill 1 hour.

Place 1 package of blackberries and pears in
container of an electric blender; cover and
process until smooth. Add remaining package of
blackberries; process until smooth. Press puree
through a fine wire-mesh strainer to remove
seeds; discard seeds. Add puree and orange juice
to sugar mixture; stir well.

Pour blackberry mixture into freezer container
of a 1-gallon hand-turned or electric freezer.

Freeze according to manufacturer's instructions. Pack freezer with additional ice and rock
salt, and let stand 1 hour. **Yield: 7½ cups.**

Blackberry Sorbet

Praline Freeze

Pralines

1½ cups sugar
¾ cup firmly packed brown sugar
¼ cup plus 2 tablespoons butter or margarine
½ cup half-and-half
2 cups pecan halves

Combine all ingredients in a large heavy saucepan. Cook over low heat, stirring gently, until sugar dissolves. Cover and cook over medium heat 2 to 3 minutes to wash sugar crystals from sides of pan.

Uncover and cook to soft ball stage (235°), stirring constantly.

Remove from heat, and beat with a wooden spoon just until mixture begins to thicken. Working rapidly, drop by tablespoonfuls onto greased wax paper; let stand until firm. **Yield: 1½ dozen.**

Royal Mocha Freeze

1 pint whipping cream
½ cup chocolate syrup
⅓ cup brandy
1 quart coffee ice cream, slightly softened
1 (6-ounce) package semisweet chocolate morsels
¾ cup chopped almonds, toasted
Garnishes: whipped cream, chocolate leaves, maraschino cherries

Beat first 3 ingredients at medium speed of an electric mixer until thickened. Place ice cream in a large plastic or metal freezer container; fold chocolate mixture into ice cream. Stir in chocolate morsels and almonds. Freeze, uncovered, about 3 hours.

Remove from freezer, and stir well. Cover and freeze.

Spoon mixture into parfait glasses, and garnish, if desired. **Yield: 8 servings.**

Praline Freeze

½ gallon vanilla ice cream, slightly softened
½ cup praline liqueur
1 cup whipping cream
2 tablespoons sugar
Pralines

Combine ice cream and liqueur in a large bowl. Spoon mixture into a 13- x 9- x 2-inch pan, and freeze.

Beat whipping cream at medium speed of an electric mixer until foamy; gradually add sugar, beating until soft peaks form.

Scoop ice cream mixture into individual compotes; sprinkle with crumbled pralines, and top with whipped cream mixture and praline pieces. **Yield: 8 servings.**

Here's the Scoop!

Ices and sorbets are frozen mixtures made from water, sugar, and a flavoring such as fruit juice or wine. An ice has a slightly grainy texture, while a sorbet is satiny smooth. Sherbet is similar but because it may contain milk, it is richer than an ice or sorbet but lighter than ice cream.

Frozen Fruit Cream

1 envelope unflavored gelatin
3 cups sugar
2 cups pineapple juice
2 cups orange juice
⅓ cup lemon juice
2 (8-ounce) packages cream cheese, softened
1 pint whipping cream, whipped
1 teaspoon almond extract
Fresh Plum Sauce

Combine first 3 ingredients in a saucepan; cook over medium heat, stirring constantly, until gelatin dissolves (about 2 minutes). Pour into a large bowl. Add orange juice and lemon juice, and set aside.

Beat cream cheese at high speed of an electric mixer until creamy. Gradually stir about one-fourth of juice mixture into cream cheese; add to remaining juice mixture, stirring constantly.

Fold whipped cream and almond extract into juice mixture.

Pour mixture into freezer container of a 1-gallon hand-turned or electric freezer.

Freeze according to manufacturer's instructions. Pack freezer with additional ice and rock salt, and let stand 1 hour. Top each serving with Fresh Plum Sauce. **Yield: 3 quarts.**

Fresh Plum Sauce

1 pound ripe plums, pitted and quartered (about 4 plums)
½ cup water
3 tablespoons sugar
¼ teaspoon ground cinnamon
3 tablespoons port or other sweet red wine

Combine first 4 ingredients in a small saucepan; bring to a boil. Reduce heat, and simmer 15 minutes or until plums are soft.

Pour mixture through a fine wire-mesh strainer into a small bowl, pressing mixture against sides of strainer with back of spoon; discard solids, and cool.

Stir in port; cover and chill. **Yield: 1¼ cups.**

Frozen Fruit Cream

Creamy Bombe with Raspberry Sauce

Creamy Bombe with Raspberry Sauce

1 (16-ounce) package frozen unsweetened
   sliced peaches, thawed and drained
1 (8-ounce) carton sour cream
½ cup grenadine
½ gallon vanilla ice cream, slightly softened
Vegetable cooking spray
Garnishes: fresh raspberries, fresh mint sprigs
Raspberry Sauce

Position knife blade in food processor bowl; add peaches, and process until smooth. Add sour cream and grenadine; process until well blended.

Combine peach mixture and ice cream; beat at low speed of an electric mixer until blended.

Pour mixture into an 11-cup mold coated with cooking spray; cover and freeze 8 hours or until mixture is firm.

Loosen edges of ice cream from mold two hours before serving, using tip of a knife. Invert mold onto a chilled serving plate. Wrap a warm towel around mold for 30 seconds. Remove towel, and firmly hold plate and mold together. Shake gently, and slowly lift off mold. Immediately return bombe to freezer. Remove from freezer just before serving.

Garnish, if desired. To serve, cut bombe into slices, and top with Raspberry Sauce. **Yield: 12 servings.**

Raspberry Sauce

1 (16-ounce) package frozen unsweetened
    raspberries, thawed and undrained
¾ cup light corn syrup
¼ cup Grand Marnier

Place raspberries in container of a food processor or electric blender. Process 1 minute or until smooth.

Press raspberry puree through a wire-mesh strainer; discard seeds. Stir syrup and Grand Marnier into puree. **Yield: 2 cups.**

Caramel-Toffee Bombe

1⅓ cups gingersnap cookie crumbs (about 20
    cookies)
¼ cup butter or margarine, melted
1 quart vanilla ice cream, slightly softened
4 (1.4-ounce) English toffee-flavored candy
    bars, crushed
Praline Sauce

Line a 2-quart bowl with heavy-duty plastic wrap. Set aside.

Combine cookie crumbs and butter; press mixture into prepared bowl. Combine ice cream and crushed candy, and spoon into bowl. Cover and freeze at least 8 hours.

Let bowl stand at room temperature 5 minutes before serving; invert onto a chilled serving plate. Carefully remove bowl and plastic wrap. Cut bombe into wedges, and serve immediately with warm Praline Sauce. **Yield: 10 to 12 servings.**

Praline Sauce

½ cup firmly packed brown sugar
½ cup half-and-half
¼ cup butter or margarine
¼ cup slivered almonds, toasted and chopped
1 teaspoon vanilla extract

Combine first 3 ingredients in a small saucepan; bring to a boil over medium heat, stirring occasionally. Boil 2 minutes, stirring occasionally.

Remove mixture from heat; stir in almonds and vanilla. **Yield: 1 cup.**

Spumoni Charlotte

20 ladyfingers, split
¼ cup amaretto
⅔ cup chocolate wafer crumbs
1 quart vanilla ice cream, slightly softened
1 tablespoon rum
1 (6-ounce) jar maraschino cherries, drained
1 quart pistachio ice cream, slightly softened
1 cup whipping cream
½ cup sifted powdered sugar
1 tablespoon rum
Garnish: maraschino cherries

Brush cut side of ladyfingers with amaretto; roll lightly in chocolate crumbs. Line bottom and sides of a 9-inch springform pan with ladyfingers.

Combine vanilla ice cream and 1 tablespoon rum; spoon into pan, spreading to sides. Place cherries over ice cream; press cherries gently. Freeze until firm.

Spoon pistachio ice cream over cherries; spread to sides. Freeze until firm.

Combine whipping cream, sugar, and 1 tablespoon rum in a mixing bowl; beat at high speed of an electric mixer until soft peaks form. Spoon cream mixture into a decorating bag fitted with large metal tip No. 2110. Remove sides of springform pan. Pipe rosettes over top and around bottom edge.

Return to freezer until ready to serve. Garnish, if desired. **Yield: 10 to 12 servings.**

Layered Sherbet Dessert

Layered Sherbet Dessert

2⅔ cups chocolate wafer crumbs, divided
½ cup butter or margarine, melted
1 quart orange sherbet, slightly softened
1 quart rainbow sherbet, slightly softened
1 quart lime sherbet, slightly softened
Raspberry-Orange Sauce
Garnishes: chocolate curls, orange rind curls,
   fresh mint sprigs

Combine 1⅔ cups chocolate crumbs and butter; press onto bottom of a 10-inch springform pan. Freeze until firm.

Spread orange sherbet evenly over frozen crust. Sprinkle with ½ cup chocolate crumbs; freeze until firm. Repeat procedure with rainbow sherbet and remaining crumbs; freeze until firm.

Spread lime sherbet over frozen crumb layer. Cover and freeze at least 8 hours.

Remove sides of springform pan. Spoon 2 to 3 tablespoons Raspberry-Orange Sauce onto each serving plate. Place wedge of sherbet dessert over sauce. Garnish, if desired. **Yield: 12 to 14 servings.**

Raspberry-Orange Sauce

2 (10-ounce) packages frozen raspberries in
   light syrup, thawed
2 tablespoons frozen orange juice concentrate,
   thawed and undiluted
1 tablespoon plus 1 teaspoon cornstarch

Place raspberries in container of a food processor or electric blender. Process 1 minute or until smooth.

Press raspberry puree through a wire-mesh strainer; discard seeds. Set puree aside.

Combine orange juice concentrate and cornstarch in a saucepan; add puree, and stir well. Cook over medium heat, stirring constantly, until mixture comes to a boil. Cook 1 minute, stirring constantly. Pour sauce into a bowl. Cover and chill. **Yield: 2⅓ cups.**

Frozen Almond Crunch

⅔ cup sliced almonds
½ cup sugar
½ cup butter or margarine
1 tablespoon all-purpose flour
2 tablespoons milk
½ gallon vanilla ice cream, slightly softened
Dark Chocolate Sauce

Combine first 5 ingredients in a heavy saucepan; bring to a boil over medium heat, stirring constantly. Remove from heat, and set aside.

Line a 15- x 10- x 1-inch jellyroll pan with aluminum foil; spread almond mixture onto foil.

Bake mixture at 350° for 7 minutes or until light golden. Cool; remove from foil, and crumble.

Sprinkle half of almond mixture in a 10-inch springform pan. Spoon ice cream evenly on top; gently press remaining almond mixture on top.

Freeze 8 hours or until firm. Serve with Dark Chocolate Sauce. **Yield: 12 servings.**

Dark Chocolate Sauce

½ cup butter or margarine
4 (1-ounce) squares unsweetened chocolate
1½ cups sugar
½ cup cocoa
Pinch of salt
1 cup milk
1 teaspoon vanilla extract

Melt butter and chocolate in a heavy saucepan over low heat, stirring often.

Combine sugar, cocoa, and salt; stir sugar mixture and milk into chocolate mixture.

Bring just to a boil over medium heat, stirring constantly; remove from heat, and stir in vanilla. Cool, stirring occasionally. Sauce may be refrigerated up to 1 week. **Yield: 2½ cups.**

Note: Sauce thickens when refrigerated. To serve, microwave at HIGH, stirring at 30-second intervals, until drizzling consistency.

Frozen Viennese Torte

18 large cinnamon graham crackers
2 (2-ounce) packages slivered almonds
⅓ cup butter or margarine, cut into small
　　pieces
1 quart chocolate ice cream, slightly softened
1 quart coffee ice cream, slightly softened
1 quart vanilla ice cream, slightly softened
2½ teaspoons ground cinnamon
1 (2-ounce) package slivered almonds, toasted
Amaretto-Cinnamon Sauce

Position knife blade in food processor bowl; add graham crackers and 2 packages almonds. Process until crushed. Add butter, processing until blended.

Press mixture onto bottom and 1 inch up sides of a 10-inch springform pan. Bake at 375° for 10 minutes. Cool on a wire rack.

Spread chocolate ice cream onto bottom and 1 inch up sides of crust; freeze until firm.

Spread coffee ice cream over chocolate ice cream; freeze until firm.

Beat vanilla ice cream and cinnamon at low speed of an electric mixer until blended; spread over coffee ice cream, and freeze 8 hours.

Sprinkle each serving with toasted almonds, and drizzle with Amaretto-Cinnamon Sauce. **Yield: 12 to 14 servings.**

Amaretto-Cinnamon Sauce
¾ cup amaretto or other almond-flavored
　　liqueur
¾ cup honey
¼ teaspoon ground cinnamon

Combine all ingredients in a small saucepan; cook over medium heat until thoroughly heated, stirring often.

Remove from heat, and cool to room temperature. **Yield: 1½ cups.**

Chocolate Ice Cream Brownies

1 (23.6-ounce) package fudge brownie mix
½ gallon vanilla ice cream, slightly softened
2 cups sifted powdered sugar
⅔ cup semisweet chocolate morsels
1½ cups evaporated milk
½ cup butter or margarine
1 teaspoon vanilla extract
1½ cups chopped pecans or walnuts

Prepare brownie mix according to package directions in a lightly greased 13- x 9- x 2-inch pan. Cool in pan on a wire rack.

Spread ice cream over brownies; freeze until ice cream is firm.

Combine sugar and next 3 ingredients in a saucepan. Bring to a boil; reduce heat to medium, and cook 8 minutes. Remove from heat, and stir in vanilla and pecans. Cool. Spread frosting over ice cream. Freeze.

Remove from freezer 5 to 10 minutes before serving. Cut into squares. **Yield: 15 servings.**

Frosty Findings

• Avoid purchasing a sticky carton of sherbet or ice cream as it has likely thawed and been refrozen.

• After opening a carton of ice cream, press a sheet of plastic wrap over the unused portion before closing the carton. This helps keep ice crystals from forming.

• If ice cream is too hard to scoop, use an electric knife to cut blocks of ice cream into slices.

• To soften a quart of ice cream, microwave at MEDIUM-LOW (30% power) about 30 seconds.

Mint-Chocolate Chip Ice Cream Squares

Mint-Chocolate Chip Ice Cream Squares

3 cups cream-filled chocolate sandwich cookie
    crumbs (about 30 cookies, crushed)
¼ cup butter or margarine, melted
½ gallon mint-chocolate chip ice cream,
    slightly softened
1 (5-ounce) can evaporated milk
½ cup sugar
1½ (1-ounce) squares unsweetened chocolate
1 tablespoon butter or margarine
1 (12-ounce) carton frozen whipped topping,
    thawed
1 cup chopped pecans, toasted
Garnish: fresh mint sprigs

Combine cookie crumbs and ¼ cup butter.
Press mixture into a lightly greased 13- x 9- x 2-
inch pan; freeze until firm.

Spread ice cream evenly over crust; freeze
until firm.

Combine evaporated milk and next 3 ingredients in a small heavy saucepan. Bring to a boil
over low heat, stirring constantly with a wire
whisk. Cook, stirring constantly, 3 to 4 minutes
or until mixture thickens. Cool mixture to room
temperature.

Spread chocolate mixture over ice cream; top
with whipped topping, and sprinkle with pecans.
Freeze until firm.

Let stand 10 minutes at room temperature
before serving. Cut into squares, and garnish, if
desired. **Yield: 15 servings.**

Brownie Baked Alaska

Brownie Baked Alaska

1 **quart strawberry or vanilla ice cream**
½ **cup butter or margarine, softened**
2 **cups sugar, divided**
2 **large eggs**
1 **cup all-purpose flour**
½ **teaspoon baking powder**
¼ **teaspoon salt**
2 **tablespoons cocoa**
1 **teaspoon vanilla extract**
5 **egg whites**
½ **teaspoon cream of tartar**
Strawberry halves

Line a 1-quart freezerproof bowl (about 7 inches in diameter) with wax paper, leaving an overhang around edges. Pack ice cream into bowl, and freeze until very firm.

Beat butter at medium speed of an electric mixer until creamy. Add 1 cup sugar; beat well. Add 2 eggs, one at a time; beat after each addition.

Combine flour and next 3 ingredients. Add to butter mixture; mix well. Stir in vanilla. Pour into a greased and floured 8-inch round cakepan.

Bake at 350° for 25 to 30 minutes or until a wooden pick inserted in center comes out clean. Cool in pan on a wire rack 10 minutes. Remove from pan, and cool completely on wire rack.

Place cake on an ovenproof wooden board or serving dish. Invert ice cream onto cake, leaving wax paper intact; remove bowl. Place ice cream-topped cake in freezer.

Combine egg whites, remaining 1 cup sugar, and cream of tartar in top of a double boiler. Place over simmering water. Cook, stirring constantly with a wire whisk, 5 minutes or until mixture reaches 160°. Remove from heat. Beat at high speed 5 minutes or until soft peaks form.

Remove ice cream-topped cake from freezer, and peel off wax paper. Quickly spread meringue over entire surface, making sure edges are sealed.

Bake at 500° for 2 minutes or until meringue peaks are lightly browned. Arrange strawberry halves around edges, and serve immediately.
Yield: 10 to 12 servings.

Note: After meringue is sealed, dessert can be frozen up to 1 week; bake just before serving.

Brownie Baked Alaska Technique

Pack ice cream into a freezerproof bowl for Brownie Baked Alaska; freeze until very firm.

Fruit Finales

Fruit desserts make a spectacular presentation and, best of all, are not difficult to prepare. Most recipes take advantage of the natural beauty of fresh fruit by calling for only a few additional ingredients.

Caramel Brie with Fresh Fruit, Fantastic Ambrosia, Peach Frost

Bananas Foster, Fresh Peach Crêpes, Peaches and Cream, Blueberry Buckle

Blueberry-Lemon Napoleons, Baked Pears à la Mode, Hot Cranberry Bake

Strawberries Jamaica, Poached Pears with Dark Chocolate Sauce

Ruby Poached Pears (page 94)

Caramel Brie with Fresh Fruit

1 (15-ounce) mini Brie
2 tablespoons butter or margarine
¾ cup firmly packed brown sugar
¼ cup light corn syrup
1½ tablespoons all-purpose flour
¼ cup milk
½ cup coarsely chopped pecans, toasted
1 tablespoon lemon juice
¼ cup water
Pear and apple wedges
Grapes

Place Brie on a large serving plate.

Melt butter in a saucepan; add brown sugar, corn syrup, and flour, stirring well. Bring mixture to a boil; reduce heat, and simmer 5 minutes, stirring constantly.

Remove from heat; cool to lukewarm. Gradually stir in milk.

Pour caramel over Brie, allowing excess to drip down sides; sprinkle with pecans.

Combine lemon juice and water; toss with fruit wedges. Drain. Arrange fruit around Brie. Serve immediately. **Yield: 14 servings.**

Festive Fruit Compote

2 cups cantaloupe or honeydew melon balls
2 cups fresh strawberries, halved
2 cups fresh blueberries
3 medium bananas, sliced
1½ cups sliced fresh peaches
1 (25.4-ounce) bottle sparkling white grape juice, chilled

Layer first 3 ingredients in a bowl or compote; cover and chill until serving time.

Top with sliced bananas and peaches; pour white grape juice over top. Serve with a slotted spoon. **Yield: 8 to 10 servings.**

Layered Ambrosia

1 (6-ounce) can pineapple juice
½ cup orange juice
¼ cup sifted powdered sugar
7 large oranges
3 medium-size pink grapefruit
5 medium bananas
1 small fresh pineapple, peeled and cored
1 (3½-ounce) can flaked coconut
Garnish: maraschino cherries with stems

Combine first 3 ingredients; stir well, and set juice mixture aside.

Peel oranges; cut crosswise into ½-inch slices. Peel and section grapefruit, catching juice in a bowl.

Peel bananas, and cut diagonally into ½-inch slices. Dip banana slices in pineapple juice mixture to prevent browning, using a slotted spoon.

Cut pineapple into 1-inch chunks.

Arrange half of orange slices in a 3-quart serving bowl. Top with sliced bananas, grapefruit, half of coconut, and pineapple chunks. Top with remaining orange slices.

Pour grapefruit juice and pineapple juice mixture over fruit. Cover and chill thoroughly.

Sprinkle with remaining coconut, and garnish, if desired. **Yield: 12 servings.**

Layered Ambrosia Technique

Prepare pineapple by cutting off the leafy green top. Then trim the eyes, and remove the hard core.

Layered Ambrosia

Fantastic Ambrosia

4 bananas, sliced
¼ cup orange juice
2 cups orange sections
1 cup fresh strawberries, halved
¼ cup salad dressing or mayonnaise
1 tablespoon sugar
½ cup whipping cream, whipped
2 tablespoons flaked coconut, toasted

Toss bananas in orange juice; drain and reserve juice. Layer orange sections, bananas, and strawberries in a serving bowl; cover and chill.

Combine salad dressing, sugar, and reserved orange juice; fold in whipped cream. Spoon mixture over fruit, and sprinkle with coconut. **Yield: 6 to 8 servings.**

Bananas Foster

4 bananas
1 tablespoon lemon juice
½ cup firmly packed brown sugar
¼ cup butter or margarine
Dash of ground cinnamon
⅓ cup light rum
Coffee or vanilla ice cream

Cut bananas in half lengthwise, and toss in lemon juice; set aside.

Combine brown sugar and butter in a large skillet; cook over low heat 2 minutes, stirring constantly, until sugar melts. Add bananas; stir gently, and cook 1 to 2 minutes or until mixture is thoroughly heated. Remove from heat, and sprinkle with cinnamon.

Heat rum in a small, long-handled saucepan over medium heat (do not boil). Remove from heat. Ignite rum with a long match, and pour over banana mixture. Let flames die down. Spoon immediately over ice cream. **Yield: 4 servings.**

Blueberry-Lemon Napoleons

1 (17¼-ounce) package frozen puff pastry
   sheets, thawed
Blueberry Sauce
Lemon Filling

Unfold pastry sheets, and cut into 9 (3-inch) rounds. Place on an ungreased baking sheet.

Bake at 400° for 10 minutes or until lightly browned. Remove to a wire rack to cool. Split each round in half crosswise, forming 18 rounds.

Spoon Blueberry Sauce evenly onto 6 plates; place 1 pastry round in center of each. Spoon or pipe half of Lemon Filling evenly onto pastry rounds; top each with a second pastry round and remaining filling. Top with remaining rounds. Serve immediately. **Yield: 6 servings.**

Blueberry Sauce
2 cups fresh blueberries
¼ cup sifted powdered sugar

Position knife blade in food processor bowl; add blueberries and sugar. Process until pureed.

Pour through a wire-mesh strainer, discarding solids. **Yield: about 1 cup.**

Lemon Filling
1 (14-ounce) can sweetened condensed milk
1 (8-ounce) package cream cheese, softened
¼ cup lemon juice
½ teaspoon vanilla extract

Combine all ingredients in a small mixing bowl; beat at medium speed of an electric mixer until smooth.

Cover and chill 1 hour or until thickened. **Yield: 1¾ cups.**

Flaming Cranberry Jubilee

1 cup sugar
1 cup water
⅛ teaspoon ground cinnamon
2 cups fresh cranberries
⅓ cup chopped pecans
3 tablespoons rum
Vanilla ice cream

Combine first 3 ingredients in a saucepan. Bring mixture to a boil, stirring occasionally; boil 5 minutes.

Add cranberries, and return to a boil; cook 5 minutes, stirring occasionally. Stir in pecans. Remove from heat.

Heat rum in a small, long-handled saucepan over medium heat (do not boil). Remove from heat. Ignite rum with a long match, and pour over cranberries. Let flames die down. Spoon immediately over ice cream. **Yield: 4 to 6 servings.**

Oranges Grand Marnier

12 medium navel oranges
⅓ to ½ cup Grand Marnier or other orange-flavored liqueur
1½ quarts orange sherbet, slightly softened

Cut a ½-inch slice from the stem end of each orange. Scoop out pulp, removing membrane and seeds; reserve orange shells. Chop pulp, and drain well.

Combine orange pulp, Grand Marnier, and sherbet; stir until blended. Spoon into orange shells, and place in muffin pans. Freeze 8 hours.

Remove from freezer 20 to 30 minutes before serving. **Yield: 12 servings.**

Peaches Foster

2 tablespoons butter or margarine
¼ cup firmly packed brown sugar
4 medium peaches, peeled and sliced
Dash of ground cinnamon
2 tablespoons rum
Vanilla ice cream

Melt butter in a medium skillet; add brown sugar, and cook over medium heat until bubbly. Add peaches; heat 3 to 4 minutes, basting constantly with syrup. Stir in cinnamon.

Heat rum in a small, long-handled saucepan over medium heat (do not boil). Remove from heat. Ignite rum with a long match, and pour over peaches. Let flames die down. Spoon rum immediately over ice cream. **Yield: 6 servings.**

Peach Frost

(pictured on page 91)

3 ripe peaches, pitted, and quartered (about 1 pound)
¼ to ½ cup light corn syrup
¼ teaspoon ground ginger
1 cup pineapple or lemon sherbet
1 cup vanilla ice cream
½ cup ginger ale
Garnishes: peach slices, peach leaves

Combine first 3 ingredients in container of an electric blender; cover and process until smooth.

Add sherbet and ice cream; cover and process until smooth. Add ginger ale; blend 30 seconds. Garnish, if desired. **Yield: 4 servings.**

Berry Napoleons

Strawberries Jamaica

1 (3-ounce) package cream cheese, softened
½ cup firmly packed brown sugar
1½ cups sour cream
2 tablespoons Grand Marnier or other orange-
   flavored liqueur
1 quart fresh strawberries

Beat cream cheese at medium speed of an electric mixer until smooth. Add sugar, sour cream, and Grand Marnier; beat 1 minute or until smooth. Cover and chill. Serve as a dip with strawberries. **Yield: about 10 to 12 servings.**

Berry Napoleons

Vegetable cooking spray
1½ cups quick-cooking oats, uncooked
½ cup butter or margarine, melted
¾ cup sugar
1 teaspoon all-purpose flour
1 teaspoon baking powder
1 large egg, lightly beaten
½ cup chopped pecans
1 teaspoon vanilla extract
¾ cup semisweet chocolate morsels
1½ tablespoons Chambord or other
   raspberry-flavored liqueur
1 tablespoon butter or margarine
2 cups whipping cream
¼ cup sifted powdered sugar
1 pint fresh raspberries or blackberries
Garnish: fresh berries

Cover baking sheets with aluminum foil, and coat with cooking spray. Set aside.

Combine oats and ½ cup melted butter in a bowl; stir in sugar, flour, and baking powder. Add egg, pecans, and vanilla, stirring until blended.

Drop by rounded teaspoonfuls 2 inches apart into 36 mounds onto prepared baking sheets.

Bake at 325° for 12 minutes or until lightly browned. Cool completely on baking sheets. Remove from foil, and place on wax paper.

Combine chocolate morsels, liqueur, and 1 tablespoon butter in a small saucepan; cook mixture over low heat, stirring constantly, until chocolate melts.

Spoon mixture into a heavy-duty, zip-top plastic bag; seal. Snip a tiny hole in 1 corner of bag, and gently squeeze bag to drizzle chocolate over cooled cookies. Let stand until chocolate is firm.

Beat whipping cream until foamy; gradually add powdered sugar, beating until soft peaks form. Set aside ¾ cup whipped cream.

Place 1 cookie on each serving plate. Pipe or dollop ½-inch layer of whipped cream onto each cookie, and top with berries. Top each with a second cookie, and repeat procedure. Top with remaining cookies. Pipe or dollop with reserved ¾ cup whipped cream; top each with a berry. Garnish, if desired. **Yield: 12 servings.**

Apple Crisp

6 large cooking apples, peeled, cored, and
   sliced
½ cup sugar
¼ teaspoon ground nutmeg
¼ teaspoon ground cinnamon
1 cup all-purpose flour
1 cup firmly packed brown sugar
½ cup butter or margarine
Vanilla ice cream (optional)

Place apple slices in a lightly greased 13- x 9- x 2-inch baking dish. Combine ½ cup sugar, nutmeg, and cinnamon; sprinkle over apple.

Combine flour and brown sugar; cut in butter with a pastry blender until mixture is crumbly. Sprinkle over apple.

Bake, uncovered, at 300° for 1 hour. Serve warm with ice cream, if desired. **Yield: 8 servings.**

Sugar-Crusted Apples in Walnut-Phyllo Baskets

Sugar-Crusted Apples in Walnut-Phyllo Baskets

¼ cup lemon juice
2 cups water
6 large Granny Smith apples, peeled and
  cored
⅔ cup sugar
⅓ cup all-purpose flour
½ teaspoon ground cinnamon
⅓ cup butter or margarine
1 large egg, lightly beaten
1¼ to 1½ cups orange juice, divided
Walnut-Phyllo Baskets
Sifted powdered sugar
Garnish: fresh mint leaves

Combine lemon juice and water in a large bowl; add apples, tossing to coat well, and set aside.

Combine sugar, flour, and cinnamon; cut in butter with a pastry blender until mixture is crumbly.

Drain apples; pat dry. Brush top half of each apple with egg, and dredge in sugar mixture; place in a lightly greased 13- x 9- x 2-inch baking dish.

Spoon remaining sugar mixture into apple cavities. Pour ¾ cup orange juice over apples.

Bake at 350° for 1 hour or until tender. Remove apples; reserve pan drippings in baking dish. Place each apple in a Walnut-Phyllo Basket.

Add enough of remaining ½ to ¾ cup orange juice to pan drippings, stirring constantly, until sauce is desired consistency; spoon over apples. Sprinkle with powdered sugar, and garnish, if desired. Serve immediately. **Yield: 6 servings.**

Walnut-Phyllo Baskets
1¼ cups finely chopped walnuts
⅓ cup sugar
1¼ teaspoons grated lemon rind
1 teaspoon ground cinnamon
12 sheets frozen phyllo pastry, thawed
Vegetable cooking spray

Combine first 4 ingredients in a small bowl; set aside.

Place phyllo sheets on a damp towel. Using kitchen shears, cut phyllo lengthwise in half, and cut each portion crosswise in half, forming 48 rectangles. Place rectangles on a damp towel. (Keep phyllo covered with a damp towel.)

Spray 6 rectangles with cooking spray, and place 1 rectangle in each lightly greased 10-ounce custard cup. Repeat procedure 3 times, placing each rectangle at alternating angles.

Spoon about 1½ tablespoons walnut mixture into each shell; top each with 2 phyllo rectangles coated with cooking spray, alternating angles. Repeat procedure with remaining walnut mixture and phyllo rectangles.

Bake at 350° for 20 to 25 minutes or until golden. Gently remove shells from custard cups, and cool on wire racks. **Yield: 6 baskets.**

Note: To store any leftover thawed phyllo, wrap phyllo sheets in plastic wrap, and place in an airtight container; refreeze.

Pick an Apple

• Choose apples that have good color and smooth skin without bruises.
• For cooking or baking, select one of the following apple varieties: Granny Smith, McIntosh, Rome Beauty, Stayman, Winesap, or York Imperial.

Blueberry Buckle

½ cup shortening
¼ cup sugar
1 large egg
1 cup all-purpose flour
2 teaspoons baking powder
¼ teaspoon salt
½ cup milk
1 (16-ounce) package frozen blueberries,
    thawed and drained
2 teaspoons lemon juice
½ cup all-purpose flour
¼ cup sugar
½ teaspoon ground cinnamon
¼ cup butter or margarine

Beat shortening and ¼ cup sugar at medium speed of an electric mixer until fluffy; add egg, and beat well.

Combine 1 cup flour, baking powder, and salt; add to shortening mixture alternately with milk, beginning and ending with flour mixture. Beat until blended after each addition. Spread batter into a greased 9-inch square pan.

Combine blueberries and lemon juice; sprinkle over batter.

Combine ½ cup flour, ¼ cup sugar, and cinnamon; cut in butter with a pastry blender until mixture is crumbly. Sprinkle over blueberries.

Bake at 350° for 45 to 55 minutes or until a wooden pick inserted in center comes out clean. Serve warm. **Yield: 9 servings.**

Hot Cranberry Bake

4 cups peeled chopped cooking apple
2 cups fresh cranberries
1½ teaspoons lemon juice
1 cup sugar
1⅓ cups quick-cooking oats, uncooked
1 cup chopped walnuts
⅓ cup firmly packed brown sugar
½ cup butter or margarine, melted
Vanilla ice cream

Layer apple and cranberries in a lightly greased 2-quart baking dish. Sprinkle with lemon juice; spoon sugar over fruit. Set aside.

Combine oats and next 3 ingredients; stir just until dry ingredients are moistened and mixture is crumbly. Sprinkle over fruit.

Bake, uncovered, at 325° for 1 hour. Serve warm with ice cream. **Yield: 8 servings.**

Cranberry Criteria

• Select fresh cranberries ranging from light to dark red. A 12-ounce bag equals 3 cups berries.
• Store cranberries in original airtight package in refrigerator up to 2 weeks; freeze up to 1 year.
• Rinse frozen cranberries in cold water and drain. Stir frozen cranberries into any recipe; do not thaw berries before using.

Hot Cranberry Bake

Crêpes Suzette

Crêpes Suzette

1 cup all-purpose flour
1 teaspoon sugar
⅛ teaspoon salt
1¼ cups milk
½ teaspoon vanilla extract
2 large eggs
1 tablespoon butter or margarine, melted
Vegetable oil
2 cups orange juice
2 tablespoons cornstarch
¼ cup orange marmalade
1 tablespoon butter or margarine
1 tablespoon grated orange rind
2 medium oranges, peeled and sectioned
¼ cup Grand Marnier or other orange-
   flavored liqueur
2 tablespoons light rum
Powdered sugar (optional)

Combine first 5 ingredients in a medium bowl, beating at medium speed of an electric mixer until smooth. Add eggs, and beat well; stir in 1 tablespoon melted butter. Cover and chill batter 1 hour. (This allows flour particles to swell and soften so crêpes are light in texture.)

Brush bottom of a 6-inch crêpe pan or heavy skillet with oil; place over medium heat just until hot, not smoking.

Pour 2 tablespoons batter into pan; quickly tilt pan in all directions so batter covers bottom of pan. Cook 1 minute or until crêpe can be shaken loose from pan. Turn crêpe over, and cook about 30 seconds. (This side is usually spotty brown.)

Place crêpe on a towel to cool. Repeat with remaining batter.

Stack crêpes between sheets of wax paper to prevent sticking.

Combine orange juice and cornstarch, stirring well; pour into a chafing dish or large skillet. Add orange marmalade, 1 tablespoon butter, and orange rind; stir well.

Cook over medium heat until mixture comes to a boil, stirring constantly; boil 1 minute. Gently stir in orange sections, and cool slightly.

Dip both sides of each crêpe in orange sauce; fold in half, and then in half again. Arrange crêpes in any remaining sauce; cook over low heat until thoroughly heated.

Heat liqueur and rum in a small saucepan over medium heat (do not boil). Quickly pour over crêpes, and immediately ignite with a long match. Serve after flames die down. Sprinkle each serving with powdered sugar, if desired. **Yield: 8 servings.**

Crêpes Suzette Techniques

Lift edges to test crêpes for doneness. Crêpes are ready for turning when they can be shaken loose from pan.

Dip both sides of crêpes in orange sauce; fold crêpes in half, and then in half again. Arrange crêpes in sauce.

Fresh Peach Crêpes

2 (8-ounce) packages cream cheese, softened
½ cup sugar
2 teaspoons vanilla extract
Crêpes
6 large ripe peaches, peeled and sliced
½ cup butter or margarine, softened
½ cup firmly packed light brown sugar
1 cup whipping cream
2 tablespoons powdered sugar

Beat first 3 ingredients at medium speed of an electric mixer until smooth. Spread about 3 tablespoons mixture over each crêpe. Place peaches down center of each crêpe.

Dot peaches in each crêpe with 1 tablespoon butter, and sprinkle with 1 tablespoon brown sugar. Roll up crêpes, and place in a 13- x 9- x 2-inch baking dish; bake at 325° for 8 to 10 minutes.

Beat whipping cream and powdered sugar at medium speed until firm peaks form. Place crêpes on serving dishes; top with whipped cream. Serve immediately. **Yield: 8 servings.**

Crêpes
¾ cup all-purpose flour
¾ cup milk
2 large eggs
1 tablespoon light brown sugar
1 tablespoon vegetable oil
Dash of ground cinnamon
Dash of ground nutmeg
Dash of ground ginger
Vegetable oil

Combine first 8 ingredients in container of an electric blender; process 1 minute, stopping once to scrape down sides. Process 15 additional seconds. Cover; chill batter 1 hour.

Brush bottom of an 8-inch crêpe pan or non-stick skillet with oil; place over medium heat until hot, not smoking.

Pour about 3 tablespoons batter into pan; quickly tilt in all directions so batter covers bottom. Cook 1 minute or until crêpe can be shaken loose. Turn crêpe over; cook about 30 seconds.

Place crêpe on a towel to cool. Repeat with remaining batter. Stack crêpes between sheets of wax paper to prevent sticking. **Yield: 8 crêpes.**

Peach Cardinale

4 fresh peaches
3 cups water
1 cup sugar
1 tablespoon vanilla extract
1 (10-ounce) package frozen raspberries, thawed
1 tablespoon sugar
2 teaspoons cornstarch
¼ cup water
½ cup whipping cream, whipped
Garnish: fresh mint leaves

Place peaches in boiling water for 20 seconds. Remove peaches, and plunge into ice water. Remove skins. Cut peaches in half.

Combine 3 cups water and 1 cup sugar in a Dutch oven; bring to a boil, and cook 3 minutes, stirring occasionally. Reduce heat to low; add peach halves and vanilla.

Simmer, uncovered, 10 to 15 minutes or until tender. Chill in syrup 1 hour or up to 2 days.

Puree raspberries. Press pureed raspberries through a fine wire-mesh strainer; discard seeds.

Combine 1 tablespoon sugar and cornstarch; stir in ¼ cup water. Add to puree, stirring well.

Cook over medium heat until mixture boils. Boil 1 minute, stirring constantly. Cover; chill.

Spoon whipped cream into 4 dessert dishes. Put 2 peach halves together; place on top of cream in each dish. Pour about ¼ cup sauce around each peach. Garnish, if desired. **Yield: 4 servings.**

From front: Peach Cardinale and Peach Frost (page 81)

Peaches and Cream

1½ cups all-purpose flour
2 tablespoons sugar
½ teaspoon baking powder
½ teaspoon salt
½ cup butter or margarine
6 peaches, peeled and halved
1 cup sugar
1 teaspoon ground cinnamon
2 egg yolks
1 cup whipping cream
Vanilla ice cream

Combine first 4 ingredients; cut in butter with a pastry blender until mixture is crumbly. Press into bottom and 1 inch up sides of an 8-inch square pan.

Arrange peaches, cut side down, over crust. Combine 1 cup sugar and 1 teaspoon ground cinnamon; sprinkle over peaches.

Bake at 400° for 15 minutes.

Combine egg yolks and whipping cream; pour over peaches. Bake 30 additional minutes. Serve warm with ice cream. **Yield: 6 servings.**

Baked Pears à la Mode

2 (16-ounce) cans pear halves, drained
½ cup honey
½ cup butter or margarine, melted
1 cup crumbled almond or coconut
    macaroons or amaretto cookies
Vanilla ice cream

Arrange pears in an 11- x 7- x 1½-inch baking dish. Set aside.

Combine honey and butter; pour over pears.

Bake at 350° for 20 minutes. Sprinkle cookie crumbs over pears; bake 10 additional minutes. Serve warm with ice cream. **Yield: 6 servings.**

Poached Pears
with Dark Chocolate Sauce

½ cup water
¼ cup brandy
¼ cup sugar
1 tablespoon grated orange rind
2 tablespoons grated fresh gingerroot
4 whole black peppercorns
4 firm ripe pears with stems
⅓ cup lemon juice
2 (1-ounce) squares semisweet chocolate
2 tablespoons whipping cream
1 tablespoon light corn syrup
1 tablespoon Grand Marnier or brandy
½ teaspoon vanilla extract

Combine first 6 ingredients in a 3-quart baking dish. Microwave at HIGH 1 to 2 minutes or until sugar dissolves.

Peel pears; core from the bottom, cutting to, but not through, the stem end, leaving stems intact. Baste pears with lemon juice.

Place pears, on their sides, in brandy mixture. Cover tightly with heavy-duty plastic wrap; fold back a small edge of wrap to allow steam to escape. Microwave at HIGH 4 minutes.

Uncover, baste pears with brandy mixture, and turn them over. Cover and microwave at HIGH 3 to 5 minutes or until tender. (A sharp knife should pierce the fruit as it would room-temperature butter, yet fruit should retain its shape.)

Cool pears in liquid, turning and basting once. Place pears in serving dishes.

Place chocolate in a 1-quart glass bowl. Microwave at MEDIUM (50% power) 2 to 3 minutes or until melted, stirring every minute. Cool slightly.

Add whipping cream and next 3 ingredients, stirring until smooth. Spoon sauce over pears. **Yield: 4 servings.**

Poached Pears with Dark Chocolate Sauce

Ruby Poached Pears

(pictured on page 77)

4 large, ripe pears with stems
Lemon juice
2 cups water
½ cup grenadine syrup
½ cup sugar
½ (10-ounce) package frozen raspberries,
     thawed
Custard Sauce
Garnish: fresh mint sprigs

Peel pears; core from the bottom, cutting to, but not through, the stem end, leaving stems intact. Brush pears with lemon juice.

Combine water, grenadine, and sugar in a large saucepan; bring to a boil. Add pears, standing them upright; cover, reduce heat, and simmer 15 to 20 minutes or until pears are tender, basting often with syrup. Remove from heat.

Transfer cooked pears and syrup to a medium bowl. Cover and chill thoroughly, turning pears occasionally.

Puree raspberries. Press pureed raspberries through a fine wire-mesh strainer; discard seeds.

Spoon ¼ cup Custard Sauce onto each of 4 dessert plates. Place a chilled pear in sauce on each plate. Discard syrup.

Spoon raspberry puree in small circles over custard around each pear. Pull a wooden pick or the tip of a knife continuously through raspberry circles surrounding each pear. Garnish, if desired. **Yield: 4 servings.**

Custard Sauce
¾ cup half-and-half
½ cup milk
1 vanilla bean, split lengthwise
⅓ cup sugar
3 egg yolks
½ teaspoon cornstarch
⅛ teaspoon salt

Combine first 3 ingredients in a heavy saucepan, and simmer over medium heat. Remove and discard vanilla bean.

Beat sugar and egg yolks until thick and pale. Stir in cornstarch. Gradually add one-fourth of hot milk mixture to yolk mixture, stirring constantly. Add to remaining hot mixture, stirring constantly.

Cook mixture over medium-low heat, stirring constantly, until thickened (about 10 minutes). Remove from heat, and stir in salt. Cover and chill custard thoroughly. **Yield: 1 cup.**

Note: You may substitute vanilla extract for vanilla bean. Stir 1 teaspoon vanilla extract into custard when adding salt.

Ruby Poached Pears Techniques

Puree thawed raspberries; press pureed raspberries through a small strainer, reserving thin puree. Discard raspberry seeds.

Spoon circles of raspberry mixture over custard, using a tiny spoon. Pull a knife through the circles to create a design.

Custards & Puddings

Light and airy or smooth and creamy, these rich-tasting treats belie their humble origins. You'll be surprised at how the simplest of ingredients can be combined to create family favorites or dazzling company desserts.

Bavarian Cream with Raspberry Sauce, Orange Chiffon Dessert

Apple-Nut Rice Pudding, Buttermilk Bread Pudding with Butter-Rum Sauce

Chocolate Mousse au Grand Marnier, Charlotte Russe with Strawberry Sauce

Pineapple Angel Food Trifle, Soufflé au Chocolate Cointreau

Grand Marnier Soufflés (page 110)

Butterscotch Mousse

Bavarian Cream
with Raspberry Sauce

1½ cups sugar
2 envelopes unflavored gelatin
1 cup cold water
1 pint whipping cream
3 (8-ounce) cartons sour cream
2 teaspoons vanilla extract
Raspberry Sauce

Combine sugar and gelatin in a saucepan; add water, and stir well. Let stand 1 minute. Cook over medium heat, stirring constantly, until gelatin dissolves. Stir in whipping cream, and set aside.

Combine sour cream and vanilla in a large bowl. Whisk in whipping cream mixture until blended. Pour into a lightly oiled 7-cup mold. Cover; chill 8 hours. Unmold onto serving dish; spoon sauce over top. **Yield: 12 servings.**

Raspberry Sauce

1 (10-ounce) package frozen raspberries, thawed
2 tablespoons sugar
1 tablespoon raspberry-flavored liqueur

Combine all ingredients in container of an electric blender; cover, and process until smooth. Press mixture through a fine wire-mesh strainer; discard seeds. **Yield: ¾ cup.**

Butterscotch Mousse

2½ cups butterscotch morsels
1 tablespoon shortening
½ cup sugar
¼ cup water
4 egg whites
1 pint whipping cream
1 teaspoon vanilla extract
Garnish: white chocolate and chocolate curls

Melt butterscotch morsels and shortening in a heavy saucepan over low heat, stirring frequently. Remove from heat; set aside, and keep warm.

Combine sugar and water in a small saucepan; cook over medium heat, stirring gently, until sugar dissolves. Cook, without stirring, to soft ball stage (240°). Remove from heat.

Beat egg whites in a large mixing bowl at high speed of an electric mixer until soft peaks form. Pour hot sugar mixture in a heavy stream over egg whites, beating constantly at high speed until thickened.

Fold in butterscotch mixture. Cool to room temperature.

Beat whipping cream at medium speed until soft peaks form; gently fold whipped cream into butterscotch mixture. Fold in vanilla.

Spoon mousse into dessert dishes. Cover and chill. Garnish, if desired. **Yield: 8 servings.**

Chocolate Mousse
au Grand Marnier

1 (4-ounce) package sweet baking chocolate
4 (1-ounce) squares semisweet chocolate
¼ cup Grand Marnier or other orange-flavored liqueur
1 pint whipping cream
½ cup sifted powdered sugar
Garnish: chocolate curls

Combine first 3 ingredients in a heavy saucepan; cook over low heat until chocolate melts, stirring constantly. Remove from heat, and cool to lukewarm.

Beat whipping cream at medium speed of an electric mixer until foamy; gradually add powdered sugar, beating until soft peaks form. Gently fold about one-fourth of whipped cream into chocolate; fold in remaining whipped cream.

Spoon into individual serving dishes. Cover; chill. Garnish, if desired. **Yield: 6 servings.**

Almond Cream
with Fresh Strawberries

1 quart fresh strawberries
⅓ cup amaretto
⅔ cup water
2 to 2½ dozen ladyfingers
1 cup butter or margarine, softened
1 cup sugar
½ cup amaretto
¼ teaspoon almond extract
1⅓ cups finely chopped almonds, toasted
1 pint whipping cream
Strawberry Sauce

Wash and hull strawberries; drain well. Set aside.

Line bottom and sides of a 3-quart glass bowl or mold with wax paper. Combine ⅓ cup amaretto and ⅔ cup water in a small bowl; mix well. Brush over ladyfingers.

Beat butter and sugar at high speed of an electric mixer until fluffy. Add ½ cup amaretto and almond extract, mixing well. Fold in almonds.

Beat whipping cream at medium speed until soft peaks form; fold into butter mixture.

Line bottom and sides of bowl or mold with ladyfingers. Arrange about 10 strawberries between ladyfingers. Layer half each of whipped cream mixture, strawberries, and ladyfingers. Repeat layers. Cover bowl with wax paper. Place a plate over bowl; chill 8 hours or overnight.

Unmold and remove wax paper; serve with Strawberry Sauce. **Yield: 12 servings.**

Strawberry Sauce

2 cups fresh strawberries
¼ to ⅓ cup sugar
1½ tablespoons kirsch
½ teaspoon lemon juice

Wash and hull strawberries; drain well. Puree strawberries in blender. Add remaining ingredients; mix well. **Yield: 1¾ cups.**

Island Trifle

6 large eggs, beaten
¾ cup sugar
6 cups half-and-half
1½ teaspoons vanilla extract
1 (16-ounce) frozen pound cake, thawed and cut into ½-inch cubes
3 to 4 tablespoons bourbon, divided
2 Red Delicious apples, unpeeled, cored, and chopped
2 cups seedless green grapes, halved

Combine eggs and sugar in a heavy saucepan; gradually stir in half-and-half. Cook over medium heat, stirring constantly with a wire whisk, until mixture thickens and coats a spoon (about 30 minutes). Stir in vanilla.

Place half of cake in bottom of a 16-cup trifle bowl; sprinkle with 1½ tablespoons bourbon. Pour half of custard over cake. Repeat procedure with remaining cake, bourbon, and custard. Cover and chill 3 to 4 hours.

Combine chopped apple and grapes; serve with trifle. **Yield: 12 to 15 servings.**

Apricot Mousse

20 ladyfingers
3 (16-ounce) cans apricot halves, undrained
2 envelopes unflavored gelatin
5 egg yolks
1¼ cups sugar, divided
⅛ teaspoon salt
1 cup milk
2 tablespoons apricot brandy or light rum
1 (2-ounce) package slivered almonds
2¼ cups whipping cream, divided
2 tablespoons powdered sugar
⅛ teaspoon almond extract
Garnishes: apricots, fresh mint, sliced toasted almonds

Apricot Mousse and Pumpkin Roll (page 43)

Cut a 30- x 3-inch strip of wax paper; line sides of a 9-inch springform pan with strip. Split ladyfingers in half lengthwise; line sides and bottom of pan with ladyfingers.

Drain apricots, reserving ½ cup juice. Set aside 4 apricots for garnish. Place knife blade in food processor bowl; add remaining apricots, and process 1 minute. Set aside.

Sprinkle gelatin over reserved ½ cup apricot juice. Set aside.

Combine egg yolks, ¾ cup sugar, and salt in a saucepan. Gradually add milk; cook over medium heat, stirring constantly, about 4 minutes or until mixture thickens and thermometer registers 160°.

Add softened gelatin, stirring mixture until gelatin dissolves. Stir in pureed apricots, brandy, and slivered almonds. Chill mixture until the consistency of unbeaten egg white (about 30 minutes).

Beat 1½ cups whipping cream at medium speed of an electric mixer until foamy; gradually add remaining ½ cup sugar, beating until soft peaks form. Fold whipped cream into apricot mixture; spoon into springform pan. Cover and chill 8 hours.

Remove sides of springform pan; remove wax paper. Beat remaining ¾ cup whipping cream until foamy; gradually add powdered sugar and almond extract, beating until soft peaks form. Pipe or dollop on top of mousse.

Slice reserved apricots; arrange on whipped cream. Garnish, if desired. **Yield: 8 to 10 servings.**

Charlotte Russe
with Strawberry Sauce

2 envelopes unflavored gelatin
¼ cup cold water
⅔ cup sugar
4 egg yolks
1⅓ cups milk
1 teaspoon vanilla extract
½ cup sour cream
⅓ cup chopped almonds, toasted
1 cup whipping cream, whipped
16 ladyfingers, split
Strawberry Sauce

Sprinkle gelatin over cold water; let stand 1 minute. Set aside.

Combine sugar and egg yolks in a heavy saucepan; beat at medium speed of an electric mixer until thick and pale. Add milk, and cook over medium heat, stirring constantly, until thermometer registers 160° (about 5 minutes).

Add reserved gelatin mixture, stirring until gelatin dissolves. Stir in vanilla, sour cream, and almonds; cool slightly. Fold in whipped cream.

Line a 2-quart mold with 20- x 2-inch strips of wax paper, slightly overlapping. Line sides and bottom of mold with ladyfingers. Spoon cream mixture over ladyfingers. Arrange remaining ladyfingers over cream mixture. Cover and chill at least 8 hours. Invert mold, and remove dessert. Carefully peel off wax paper. Serve with Strawberry Sauce. **Yield: 8 to 10 servings.**

Strawberry Sauce
1 pint fresh strawberries
1 tablespoon lemon juice
½ cup sugar
2 tablespoons framboise or other raspberry brandy

Wash and hull strawberries; drain well. Put in container of an electric blender. Cover; process until smooth. Add lemon juice and remaining ingredients; blend until smooth. **Yield: 1⅓ cups.**

Orange Chiffon Dessert

2 (3-ounce) packages ladyfingers
3 to 4 tablespoons Grand Marnier or other orange-flavored liqueur
3 envelopes unflavored gelatin
1¾ cups cold water, divided
1 cup sugar
3 oranges, peeled, seeded, and sectioned
1 tablespoon grated orange rind
1¾ cups fresh orange juice
2 tablespoons fresh lemon juice
1¾ cups whipping cream
¾ cup miniature marshmallows
¼ cup chopped pecans, toasted
Garnishes: orange sections, fresh mint leaves

Cut a 30- x 3-inch strip of wax paper; line sides of a 9-inch springform pan with strip. Split ladyfingers in half lengthwise; line sides and bottom of pan with ladyfingers. Brush ladyfingers with liqueur. Set aside.

Sprinkle gelatin over ¾ cup cold water; stir and let stand 1 minute.

Combine remaining 1 cup water and sugar in a saucepan; bring to a boil, stirring until sugar dissolves. Add gelatin, stirring until it dissolves.

Chop orange sections; drain on paper towels. Stir oranges and next 3 ingredients into gelatin mixture. Chill until consistency of unbeaten egg white (about 30 minutes).

Beat whipping cream at medium speed of an electric mixer until soft peaks form. Fold whipped cream and marshmallows into orange mixture. Spoon into prepared pan, and sprinkle with pecans. Cover and chill 8 hours.

Remove sides of springform pan; remove wax paper. Place on serving plate, and garnish, if desired. **Yield: 10 to 12 servings.**

Orange Chiffon Dessert

Special Strawberry Trifle

Pineapple Angel Food Trifle

1 (16-ounce) can pineapple tidbits, undrained
2 (3.4-ounce) packages vanilla instant
    pudding mix
3 cups milk
1 (8-ounce) carton sour cream
1 (10-inch) angel food cake, cut into 1-inch
    cubes
1 (8-ounce) carton frozen whipped topping,
    thawed
Garnishes: mint leaves, pineapple slices

Drain pineapple tidbits, reserving 1 cup juice; set aside.

Combine pudding mix, ½ cup reserved juice, and milk in a mixing bowl; beat at low speed of an electric mixer 2 minutes or until thickened. Fold in sour cream and pineapple tidbits.

Place one-third of cake cubes in bottom of a 16-cup trifle bowl; drizzle with 2 to 3 tablespoons remaining reserved pineapple juice. Spoon one-third of pudding mixture over cake. Repeat procedure twice, ending with pudding mixture. Cover and chill at least 3 hours.

Spread top with whipped topping just before serving. Garnish, if desired. **Yield: 12 servings.**

Special Strawberry Trifle

5 cups sliced fresh strawberries, divided
2 (10¾-ounce) loaves angel food cake, cut into
    1-inch cubes
¼ cup plus 2 tablespoons strawberry-flavored
    liqueur, divided
Custard
½ cup strawberry preserves
1 pint whipping cream
¼ cup sifted powdered sugar
2 teaspoons strawberry-flavored liqueur
Garnishes: strawberry fans, toasted slivered
    almonds

Arrange enough strawberry slices, cut side down, to line the lower edge of a 14-cup trifle bowl. Arrange half of cake cubes in bowl. Sprinkle with 2 tablespoons liqueur.

Combine remaining strawberry slices and 2 tablespoons liqueur; let stand 30 minutes. Drain strawberries, reserving 2 tablespoons liquid.

Top cake with half of strawberries. Spoon 2 cups chilled Custard over strawberries. Top with remaining cake cubes; sprinkle with remaining 2 tablespoons liqueur. Spoon remaining strawberries over cake cubes.

Combine preserves and reserved strawberry liquid, stirring well; spread over strawberries. Spoon remaining Custard over preserves.

Beat whipping cream at medium speed of an electric mixer until foamy; gradually add powdered sugar, beating until soft peaks form. Add 2 teaspoons liqueur, and beat well; spread sweetened whipped cream over trifle. Garnish, if desired. Serve immediately. **Yield: 14 servings.**

Custard

1¾ cups milk, divided
¼ cup plus 2 teaspoons cornstarch
2 cups half-and-half
4 egg yolks
¾ cup sugar
2 teaspoons vanilla extract

Combine ½ cup milk and cornstarch in a large saucepan; stir well. Add remaining 1¼ cups milk and half-and-half. Cook over medium heat until thickened, stirring constantly. Set aside.

Beat egg yolks and sugar at medium speed of an electric mixer until thickened. Gradually stir about one-fourth of hot mixture into yolk mixture; add to remaining hot mixture, stirring constantly. Cook over low heat, stirring constantly, 1 to 2 minutes or until mixture thickens.

Remove from heat; stir in vanilla. Cool; cover and chill thoroughly. **Yield: 4 cups.**

Apple-Nut Rice Pudding

1 cup short-grain rice, uncooked
1 teaspoon salt
1 teaspoon butter or margarine
2 cups hot water
½ cup firmly packed brown sugar
2 tablespoons cornstarch
½ teaspoon ground cinnamon
2 cups milk
½ cup raisins
1 teaspoon vanilla extract
½ teaspoon grated lemon rind
2 egg yolks, lightly beaten
Apple-Nut Sauce

Combine rice, salt, and butter in a 2-quart baking dish; stir in hot water. Cover and microwave at HIGH 5 minutes; stir well. Cover and microwave at MEDIUM (50% power) 13 to 15 minutes or until water is absorbed; set aside.

Combine brown sugar, cornstarch, and cinnamon in a 1½-quart baking dish. Stir in milk and next 3 ingredients. Add reserved rice; stir well.

Cover; microwave at HIGH 6 minutes or until slightly thickened, stirring every 1½ minutes. Stir about 3 tablespoons of hot mixture into yolks; add to remaining hot mixture, stirring constantly.

Cover and microwave at HIGH 6 minutes or until thickened, stirring after every minute. Let stand, covered, 2 minutes.

Spoon into individual dessert bowls. Top each with warm Apple-Nut Sauce. **Yield: 6 servings.**

Apple-Nut Sauce

1 (20-ounce) can sliced cooking apples
½ cup firmly packed brown sugar
1½ tablespoons cornstarch
1 teaspoon ground cinnamon
⅛ teaspoon salt
⅓ cup chopped pecans, toasted
⅓ cup raisins
1 tablespoon butter or margarine, melted

Drain apples, reserving liquid. Add water to liquid to measure ¾ cup. Set aside.

Combine sugar and next 3 ingredients in a 4-cup glass measure; stir well. Stir in reserved liquid. Microwave, uncovered, at HIGH 5 minutes or until thickened, stirring after every minute.

Add apples, pecans, raisins, and butter; stir well. Microwave, uncovered, at HIGH 2 minutes or until mixture is thoroughly heated, stirring after every minute. **Yield: 3½ cups.**

Banana Pudding

⅔ cup sugar
3½ tablespoons all-purpose flour
Dash of salt
1 (14-ounce) can sweetened condensed milk
2½ cups milk
4 large eggs, separated
2 teaspoons vanilla extract
1 (12-ounce) package vanilla wafers
6 large bananas
¼ cup plus 2 tablespoons sugar
½ teaspoon banana or vanilla extract

Combine first 3 ingredients in a saucepan. Combine milks and yolks; add to dry ingredients.

Cook over medium heat, stirring constantly, until smooth and thickened. Remove from heat; stir in 2 teaspoons vanilla.

Arrange one-third of wafers in bottom of a 3-quart baking dish. Slice 2 bananas, and layer over wafers. Pour one-third of pudding mixture over bananas. Repeat layers twice, arranging remaining wafers around outside edge of dish.

Beat egg whites at high speed of an electric mixer until soft peaks form. Add ¼ cup plus 2 tablespoons sugar, 1 tablespoon at a time, beating until stiff peaks form and sugar dissolves. Fold in remaining extract. Spread over pudding, sealing to edge of dish. Bake at 325° for 25 minutes or until meringue is golden. **Yield: 8 to 10 servings.**

Banana Pudding

Tennessee Bread Pudding with Bourbon Sauce

2 cups hot water
1½ cups sugar
1 (12-ounce) can evaporated milk
4 large eggs
1 cup flaked coconut
½ cup crushed pineapple, drained
½ cup raisins
⅓ cup butter or margarine, melted
1 teaspoon vanilla extract
½ teaspoon ground nutmeg
9 slices white bread with crust, cut into
    ½-inch cubes
Bourbon Sauce

Combine water and sugar in a bowl, stirring until sugar dissolves. Add milk and eggs, stirring with a wire whisk until blended.

Stir in coconut and next 5 ingredients. Add bread cubes; let mixture stand 30 minutes, stirring occasionally. Pour into a greased 13- x 9- x 2-inch pan.

Bake at 350° for 45 minutes or until a knife inserted in center comes out clean. Serve warm with Bourbon Sauce. **Yield: 12 servings.**

Bourbon Sauce
1 cup light corn syrup
¼ cup butter or margarine
¼ cup bourbon
½ teaspoon vanilla extract

Bring corn syrup to a boil in a saucepan. Remove from heat, and cool slightly.

Stir in butter, bourbon, and vanilla with a wire whisk. Serve warm. **Yield: 1½ cups.**

Tennessee Bread Pudding with Bourbon Sauce

Bread Pudding with Whiskey Sauce

1 (1-pound) loaf French bread
2 cups half-and-half
2 cups milk
3 large eggs, lightly beaten
2 cups sugar
½ cup chopped pecans
½ cup raisins
¼ cup shredded coconut
1 tablespoon plus 1 teaspoon vanilla extract
½ teaspoon orange extract
1½ teaspoons ground cinnamon
2 tablespoons butter or margarine, melted
½ cup shredded coconut
½ cup chopped pecans
Whiskey Sauce

Break bread into small pieces, and place in a shallow bowl. Add half-and-half and milk, and let stand 10 minutes. Crush mixture with hands until blended. Add eggs and next 7 ingredients, stirring well.

Pour melted butter into a 13- x 9- x 2-inch baking dish; tilt dish to coat evenly. Spoon pudding mixture into dish.

Bake at 325° for 40 to 45 minutes or until pudding is very firm. Remove from oven. Cool.

Combine ½ cup coconut and ½ cup pecans; stir well.

Cut pudding into squares to serve. Place each square in an ovenproof dish. Place dishes on baking sheet.

Pour Whiskey Sauce evenly over squares, and sprinkle with coconut mixture. Broil 5½ inches from heat (with electric oven door partially opened) until sauce is bubbly and coconut is lightly browned. **Yield: 15 servings.**

Whiskey Sauce
1 cup butter
2 cups sifted powdered sugar
3 tablespoons bourbon
2 large eggs, beaten

Place butter in top of a double boiler; bring water to a boil. Reduce heat to low; cook until butter melts. Add sugar and bourbon, stirring until sugar dissolves.

Stir about one-fourth of hot mixture into eggs; add to remaining hot mixture in pan, stirring constantly. Cook, stirring constantly, 5 minutes or until mixture thickens. **Yield: about 2 cups.**

Buttermilk Bread Pudding with Butter-Rum Sauce

1 (16-ounce) loaf unsliced French bread
¼ cup butter or margarine
1 quart buttermilk
1 cup raisins
2 large eggs, lightly beaten
1⅓ cups firmly packed light brown sugar
1 tablespoon vanilla extract
Butter-Rum Sauce

Tear bread into 1-inch pieces; reserve 7½ cups. Set aside remaining bread for other uses.

Melt ¼ cup butter in a 13- x 9- x 2-inch pan in 350° oven.

Combine reserved bread pieces, buttermilk, and raisins in a large bowl; set aside.

Combine eggs, brown sugar, and vanilla, whisking well. Add to bread mixture, stirring gently. Pour into pan of melted butter.

Bake at 350° for 1 hour. Serve pudding warm or cold with Butter-Rum Sauce. **Yield: 10 to 12 servings.**

Butter-Rum Sauce
½ cup butter or margarine
½ cup sugar
1 egg yolk
¼ cup water
3 tablespoons rum

Combine first 4 ingredients in a small saucepan, stirring well.

Cook over medium heat, stirring constantly, until sugar dissolves and sauce begins to thicken (about 10 minutes). Stir in rum. **Yield: ¾ cup.**

Hot Chocolate Soufflé

Hot Chocolate Soufflé

Butter or margarine
2 teaspoons sugar
2 tablespoons butter or margarine
2 tablespoons all-purpose flour
1 cup half-and-half
2 teaspoons instant coffee granules
2 (1-ounce) squares unsweetened chocolate
1 (1-ounce) square semisweet chocolate
4 large eggs, separated
1 teaspoon vanilla extract
4 egg whites
½ teaspoon cream of tartar
⅔ cup sugar
Vanilla ice cream
Velvet Ganache Sauce

Butter bottom of a 2-quart soufflé dish; sprinkle with 2 teaspoons sugar. Cut a piece of aluminum foil long enough to fit around soufflé dish, allowing a 1-inch overlap; fold foil lengthwise into thirds. Lightly butter one side of foil. Wrap foil around outside of dish, buttered side against dish, allowing it to extend 3 inches above rim to form a collar; secure with string. Set aside.

Melt 2 tablespoons butter in a heavy saucepan over low heat; add flour, stirring until smooth. Cook 1 minute, stirring constantly.

Add half-and-half gradually; cook over medium heat, stirring constantly, until thickened and bubbly. Remove from heat. Add coffee granules, stirring to dissolve.

Melt chocolate in a heavy saucepan over low heat; stir into coffee mixture.

Beat egg yolks. Stir one-fourth of hot mixture into yolks; add to remaining hot mixture, stirring constantly. Add vanilla. Transfer to a large bowl.

Beat 8 egg whites in a large mixing bowl at high speed of an electric mixer until foamy. Add cream of tartar, and beat until soft peaks form. Add ⅔ cup sugar, 1 tablespoon at a time, beating until stiff peaks form and sugar dissolves.

Stir 2 tablespoons beaten egg whites into chocolate mixture. Fold egg whites into chocolate mixture, one-third at a time. Spoon into prepared dish.

Make a groove 1½ inches deep around the top in a circle (about 1¼ inches from edge of dish), using a large spoon handle.

Bake at 350° for 50 to 60 minutes or until puffed and set. Remove collar. Serve soufflé immediately with ice cream. Drizzle with warm Velvet Ganache Sauce. **Yield: 8 servings.**

Velvet Ganache Sauce
1 cup whipping cream
1 (6-ounce) package semisweet chocolate morsels

Bring whipping cream to a simmer in a heavy saucepan. Remove from heat; pour over chocolate morsels. Let stand 1 minute. Stir until chocolate melts. **Yield: 1½ cups.**

Hot Chocolate Soufflé Technique

If desired, create a puffy top hat by dragging a spoon handle through batter before baking soufflé.

Soufflé au Chocolate Cointreau

Butter or margarine
2 tablespoons sugar
¼ cup butter or margarine
1 (12-ounce) package semisweet chocolate
    morsels
¼ cup Cointreau or other orange-flavored
    liqueur
12 large eggs, separated
1½ cups sifted powdered sugar
1 teaspoon ground cinnamon
1 teaspoon cream of tartar
Powdered sugar
Chocolate Cream

Butter a 2¾-quart soufflé dish. Cut a piece of aluminum foil long enough to fit around soufflé dish, allowing a 1-inch overlap; fold foil length-wise into thirds. Lightly butter one side of foil. Wrap foil around outside of dish, buttered side against dish, allowing it to extend 3 inches above rim to form a collar; secure with string or masking tape. Add 2 tablespoons sugar, tilting prepared dish to coat sides. Set aside.

Melt ¼ cup butter and chocolate morsels in a heavy saucepan over low heat, stirring often. Cool 5 minutes; stir in Cointreau. Set aside.

Beat egg yolks; gradually add 1½ cups powdered sugar, beating until mixture is thick and pale. Stir in cinnamon and chocolate mixture. Set aside.

Beat egg whites and cream of tartar in a large mixing bowl at high speed of an electric mixer until stiff peaks form.

Stir 1½ cups egg white mixture into chocolate mixture. Fold remaining egg white mixture into chocolate mixture. Spoon into prepared dish.

Bake at 375° for 50 to 55 minutes. Sprinkle with powdered sugar, and remove collar. Serve immediately with Chocolate Cream. **Yield: 12 servings.**

Chocolate Cream

1 cup whipping cream
1 tablespoon powdered sugar
1½ teaspoons cocoa

Beat all ingredients at medium speed until soft peaks form. **Yield: 2 cups.**

Grand Marnier Soufflés

(pictured on page 95)

Butter
1 tablespoon sugar
¼ cup butter
¼ cup all-purpose flour
1 cup milk
4 egg yolks
2 tablespoons Grand Marnier or other
    orange-flavored liqueur
¾ cup sugar
2 tablespoons cornstarch
5 egg whites
1 tablespoon sugar
Custard Sauce

Butter six 6-ounce custard cups; coat bottom and sides with 1 tablespoon sugar. Set aside.

Melt ¼ cup butter in a large saucepan over low heat; add flour, stirring until smooth. Cook, stirring constantly, 1 minute. Gradually stir in milk, and cook, stirring constantly, until mixture thickens and begins to leave sides of pan.

Remove from heat, and cool 15 minutes. Add egg yolks, one at a time, beating after each addition. Stir in Grand Marnier; set aside.

Combine ¾ cup sugar and cornstarch; set aside.

Beat egg whites until foamy. Add sugar mixture, beating until stiff peaks form and sugar dissolves (2 to 4 minutes). Stir one-fourth of egg white mixture into egg yolk mixture; fold in remaining egg whites. Spoon into prepared custard cups; sprinkle evenly with 1 tablespoon sugar.

Place custard cups in a shallow pan. Add hot water to pan to depth of 1 inch.

Bake at 400° for 10 minutes.

Reduce temperature to 350°, and bake 20 to 25 additional minutes or until golden. Remove custard cups from water. Serve immediately with Custard Sauce. **Yield: 6 servings.**

Custard Sauce

½ cup sugar
2 tablespoons cornstarch
4 egg yolks
1 cup milk
2 tablespoons Grand Marnier or other
    orange-flavored liqueur
½ cup half-and-half
½ cup whipping cream, whipped

Combine sugar and cornstarch in a medium saucepan; add egg yolks, stirring until smooth. Add milk, stirring until smooth.

Cook over medium heat, stirring constantly, 10 minutes or until mixture thickens and thermometer registers 160°. Remove from heat, and cool.

Stir in Grand Marnier and half-and-half. Fold in whipped cream. Cover; chill. **Yield: 1¾ cups.**

Lemon Soufflé

Butter or margarine
2 tablespoons sugar
2 envelopes unflavored gelatin
½ cup cold water
1 teaspoon sugar
1 tablespoon grated lemon rind
¾ cup lemon juice
⅓ cup meringue powder
1½ cups sugar, divided
1 cup water
1 pint whipping cream
1 (2-ounce) package slivered almonds, toasted
    and chopped

Butter a 2-quart soufflé dish. Cut a piece of wax paper long enough to fit around soufflé dish, allowing a 1-inch overlap; fold paper lengthwise into thirds. Lightly butter one side of paper. Wrap paper around outside of dish, buttered side against dish, allowing it to extend 3 inches above rim to form a collar; secure with masking tape. Sprinkle sides of dish with 2 tablespoons sugar. Set aside.

Sprinkle gelatin over cold water in a saucepan; let stand 1 minute. Add 1 teaspoon sugar; cook over low heat, stirring until gelatin dissolves. Stir in lemon rind and juice. Set aside.

Combine meringue powder, 1 cup sugar, and water in a large bowl. Beat at high speed of an electric mixer 5 minutes. Gradually add remaining ½ cup sugar, and beat at high speed 5 minutes or until stiff peaks form. Fold in gelatin mixture.

Beat whipping cream at medium speed until soft peaks form; fold into gelatin mixture.

Pour into prepared dish, and chill 8 hours.

Remove collar, and gently pat chopped almonds around sides. **Yield: 8 to 10 servings.**

Lemon Soufflé

Old-Fashioned Stirred Custard

3 large eggs
½ cup sugar
2 tablespoons all-purpose flour
¼ teaspoon salt
3 cups milk
¾ teaspoon vanilla extract

Place eggs in top of a double boiler; beat at medium speed of an electric mixer until frothy. Combine sugar, flour, and salt; gradually add to eggs, beating until thick.

Pour milk into a medium saucepan; cook over low heat until thoroughly heated (do not boil). Gradually stir about one-fourth of hot milk into egg mixture; add remaining hot milk, stirring constantly.

Bring water in bottom of double boiler to a boil. Reduce heat to low; cook, stirring constantly, 20 to 25 minutes or until mixture thickens and coats a metal spoon.

Stir in vanilla. Serve warm, or cover and chill thoroughly. **Yield: 4 cups.**

Variations

Coffee Custard: Add 1 tablespoon instant coffee granules to milk; cook over low heat until thoroughly heated and granules dissolve. Reduce vanilla extract to ¼ teaspoon. **Yield: 4 cups.**

Orange Custard: Omit vanilla extract. Gently stir 1 teaspoon orange extract into prepared custard mixture. **Yield: 4 cups.**

Peppermint Custard: Increase flour to 2½ tablespoons. Add ¼ cup finely crushed peppermint candy to milk; cook over low heat until thoroughly heated and candy dissolves. Omit vanilla extract. **Yield: 4 cups.**

Rum Custard: Reduce vanilla extract to ½ teaspoon. Gently stir 1 teaspoon rum extract into prepared custard mixture. **Yield: 4 cups.**

Sabayon Glacé

6 egg yolks
Dash of salt
⅔ cup sugar
1 cup whipping cream
½ cup dry white wine
⅔ cup Chambord or other raspberry-flavored liqueur
1 pint whipping cream, whipped
3 to 4 kiwifruit, peeled and sliced
Garnishes: kiwifruit slices, fresh raspberries, fresh mint sprigs

Combine egg yolks and salt in a large bowl; beat at high speed of an electric mixer until blended. Add sugar, 1 tablespoon at a time, beating until mixture is thick and pale (about 5 minutes).

Heat 1 cup whipping cream, white wine, and Chambord until hot, but not boiling. With mixer running on low speed, slowly pour hot cream mixture into beaten egg mixture.

Transfer mixture to top of a double boiler; place over boiling water, and cook, stirring constantly, 20 minutes. (Mixture will thicken only slightly.) Remove from heat.

Place top of double boiler with mixture over ice water, and stir until mixture is completely cold. Fold in whipped cream. Cover and chill thoroughly. Fold glacé gently at least 4 hours before serving.

Arrange sliced kiwifruit around sides of compotes; spoon glacé into compotes. Chill desserts until ready to serve. Garnish, if desired. **Yield: 8 servings.**

Sabayon Glacé

Caramel-Crowned Flans

Caramel-Crowned Flans

¾ **cup sugar**
1 **(14-ounce) can sweetened condensed milk**
⅔ **cup milk**
2 **large eggs**
2 **egg yolks**
1 **teaspoon vanilla extract**
1 **cup sugar**
4 **to 6 drops of hot water**

Place ¾ cup sugar in a heavy saucepan; cook over medium heat, stirring constantly, until sugar melts and turns light golden.

Remove from heat; pour hot caramelized sugar evenly into 4 (10-ounce) custard cups. Cool.

Combine sweetened condensed milk and next 4 ingredients in container of an electric blender; cover and process at high speed 15 seconds. Pour evenly into custard cups.

Place custard cups in a 13- x 9- x 2-inch pan; add hot water to pan to depth of 1 inch, and cover pan with aluminum foil.

Bake at 350° for 30 minutes or until a knife inserted near center comes out clean. Remove cups from water, and cool. Cover and chill at least 8 hours.

Loosen edge of custard with a spatula; invert onto individual plates, letting caramel drizzle over the top. Set aside.

Place 1 cup sugar in a heavy saucepan; cook over medium heat, stirring constantly, until sugar melts and syrup is light golden. Stir in drops of hot water; let stand 1 minute or until syrup spins a thread when drizzled from a spoon.

Drizzle syrup, quickly wrapping threads around and over flans until a delicate web is formed. (If sugar hardens before webs are formed, place saucepan over medium heat until mixture softens.)

Chill flans, uncovered, up to 45 minutes before serving. **Yield: 4 servings.**

Note: If spiced flans are desired, add ¼ teaspoon ground cinnamon, ⅛ teaspoon ground ginger, and ⅛ teaspoon ground nutmeg to egg mixture in blender. Spices will float to the top as mixture bakes.

Caramel-Crowned Flans Technique

Cook ¾ cup sugar until melted and caramel colored; pour into custard cups, and cool. Prepare and bake mixture in custard cups as directed.

Pies & Pastries

Spectacular pies and pastries are a hallmark of Southern cooking. Whether it's a pecan tart, peach cobbler, or a meringue-topped chocolate pie, these desserts tingle the tastebuds.

American Apple Pie, Blackberry and Peach Pie, Fried Apricot Pies

Pecan Tart with Praline Cream, Vanilla Cream Pie, Raspberry-Sour Cream Pie

Lemony Cherry Pie, Strawberry-Chocolate Truffle Pie, Berry Good Lemon Tarts

Peanut Butter Pie, Carolina Sweet Potato Pie, Coffee Cream Pie

Double Pecan Pie (page 122)

American Apple Pie

2 cups all-purpose flour
1 cup firmly packed brown sugar
½ cup regular oats, uncooked
½ teaspoon salt
⅓ cup chopped pecans
¾ cup butter or margarine, melted
4 cups peeled, sliced cooking apples
¾ cup sugar
1 tablespoon cornstarch
¼ teaspoon salt
½ cup water
½ teaspoon vanilla extract
Vanilla ice cream

Combine first 5 ingredients in a large bowl; add butter, and stir until blended. Measure 1 cup firmly packed mixture; set aside for pie topping.

Press remaining oats mixture in bottom and up sides of a 9-inch deep-dish pieplate. Arrange apple slices in pieplate; set aside.

Combine ¾ cup sugar, cornstarch, and salt in a saucepan; stir in water. Cook over medium heat until mixture boils. Stir in vanilla.

Pour hot mixture evenly over apples; crumble reserved topping mixture evenly over pie.

Bake at 375° for 40 minutes, covering with foil the last 15 minutes, if necessary. Serve with ice cream. **Yield: one 9-inch pie.**

Fried Apricot Pies

1 (6-ounce) package dried apricot halves, chopped
1¼ cups water
½ cup sugar
½ teaspoon ground cinnamon
½ teaspoon ground nutmeg
1 tablespoon lemon or orange juice
1 (15-ounce) package refrigerated piecrusts
Vegetable oil
Powdered sugar

Combine apricots and 1¼ cups water in a saucepan; bring to a boil. Cover, reduce heat, and simmer 20 minutes or until tender. Drain.

Mash apricots. Stir in sugar and next 3 ingredients; set aside.

Unfold 1 piecrust, and press out fold lines. Roll piecrust to ⅛-inch thickness on a lightly floured surface. Cut into five 5-inch circles; stack circles between wax paper. Repeat procedure.

Spoon 2 tablespoons apricot mixture on half of each circle. Moisten edges with water; fold dough over apricot mixture, pressing edges to seal. Crimp edges with a fork.

Pour oil to depth of 1 inch into a heavy skillet. Fry pies in hot oil (375°) 2 minutes or until golden, turning once. Drain on paper towels. Sprinkle with powdered sugar. **Yield: 10 pies.**

Berry Basics

- Check the bottom of the container when you buy packaged berries. It should be free of stains and any mashed or moldy berries.
- Wash berries just before eating.
- To store, spread berries in a single layer in a paper towel-lined container; cover with an airtight lid or plastic wrap. Refrigerate blueberries up to 10 days, strawberries up to 3 days, and raspberries and blackberries up to 2 days.
- To freeze, place berries in a single layer on a baking sheet, and freeze until firm. Pack lightly in freezer containers; label and date them. Freeze up to 9 months.

From left: Chilled Blueberry Pie (page 133), Blackberry and Peach Pie,
Juicy Blackberry Cobbler (page 139)

Blackberry and Peach Pie

⅔ cup sugar
1½ tablespoons quick-cooking tapioca
Pinch of salt
1 teaspoon grated orange rind
2 cups fresh blackberries
2 cups sliced fresh peaches
Cream Cheese Pastry

Combine first 4 ingredients in a large bowl, mixing well. Add blackberries and peaches, tossing gently. Set aside.

Roll half of Cream Cheese Pastry to ⅛-inch thickness on a lightly floured surface. Fit into a 9-inch pieplate; trim off excess pastry along edges. Fold edges under, and flute. Spoon filling into pastry shell.

Roll remaining pastry to ⅛-inch thickness; cut pastry into ½-inch-wide strips. Twist each strip several times, and place on pie in a spiral design.

Use extra pastry to shape leaf cutouts; place cutouts on outer end of spiral.

Bake at 425° for 35 to 40 minutes or until crust is browned. **Yield: one 9-inch pie.**

Cream Cheese Pastry

2 cups all-purpose flour
½ teaspoon salt
½ cup shortening
2 (3-ounce) packages cream cheese
5 to 6 tablespoons cold water

Combine flour and salt; cut in shortening and cream cheese with a pastry blender until mixture is crumbly.

Sprinkle cold water, 1 tablespoon at a time, evenly over surface; stir with a fork until moistened. Shape into a ball; cover and chill. **Yield: pastry for one double-crust pie.**

Lemony Cherry Pie

Lemony Cherry Pie

2 (16-ounce) cans tart, red pitted cherries,
   undrained
1 cup sugar
3 tablespoons cornstarch
2 tablespoons butter or margarine
1 tablespoon lemon juice
⅛ teaspoon liquid red food coloring (optional)
1 (15-ounce) package refrigerated piecrusts
1 teaspoon all-purpose flour

Drain cherries, reserving ½ cup juice. Set both aside.

Combine sugar and cornstarch in a large saucepan; stir in reserved cherry juice. Cook over medium heat, stirring constantly, until mixture comes to a boil; boil 1 minute, stirring constantly.

Remove sugar mixture from heat, and stir in cherries, butter, lemon juice, and, if desired, food coloring; cool.

Unfold 1 piecrust, and press out fold lines; sprinkle with flour, spreading over surface. Place piecrust, floured side down, in a 9-inch pieplate; trim off excess pastry along edges. Spoon filling into pastry shell.

Roll remaining piecrust to press out fold lines. Cut into ½-inch strips. Arrange in lattice design over filling; trim strips even with edge.

Cut remaining pastry into shapes with a 1-inch cutter, if desired. Moisten edge of piecrust with water, and gently press cutouts around edge.

Bake at 375° for 30 to 35 minutes. **Yield: one 9-inch pie.**

Peachy Keen Tarts

(pictured on page 121)

Tart Pastry
1 (3-ounce) package cream cheese, softened
2 tablespoons powdered sugar
½ teaspoon grated orange rind
2 teaspoons orange juice
3 large fresh peaches
¾ cup apricot preserves
2 tablespoons Cointreau

Roll each portion of pastry to ⅛-inch thickness on a floured surface. Fit pastry into six 4-inch shallow tart pans or quiche pans. Roll over top of tart pans with a rolling pin to trim excess pastry. Prick bottom of pastry with a fork.

Bake at 450° for 10 minutes or until lightly browned. Cool.

Beat cream cheese and next 3 ingredients at medium speed of an electric mixer until blended. Spoon mixture evenly into 6 tart pans, spreading to edges.

Dip peaches in boiling water 10 seconds; drain and cool slightly. Carefully peel peaches, and cut in half lengthwise; remove pit.

Cut peaches into ⅛-inch-thick lengthwise slices, keeping slices in order as they are cut. Arrange slices over cream cheese mixture in the shape of peach halves, letting slices fan out slightly.

Heat preserves over low heat until melted. Press preserves through a wire-mesh strainer to remove lumps. Stir Cointreau into preserves, and brush liberally over peaches. **Yield: 6 servings.**

Tart Pastry
1½ cups all-purpose flour
½ teaspoon baking powder
½ teaspoon salt
¼ cup butter or margarine
¼ cup shortening
4 to 6 tablespoons milk

Combine first 3 ingredients; cut in butter and shortening with a pastry blender until mixture is crumbly.

Sprinkle milk, 1 tablespoon at a time, evenly over surface; stir with a fork until dry ingredients are moistened. Divide into 6 equal portions. Wrap in plastic wrap; cover and chill. **Yield: pastry for six 4-inch tarts.**

Strawberry-Chocolate Truffle Pie

1 (6-ounce) package semisweet chocolate morsels
1 (8-ounce) package cream cheese, cubed
2 tablespoons butter or margarine
¼ cup sifted powdered sugar
3 tablespoons Triple Sec or orange juice
1 baked 9-inch pastry shell
3 to 4 cups fresh strawberries, hulled
¼ cup red currant jelly, melted
½ cup whipping cream
2 tablespoons powdered sugar
½ teaspoon grated orange rind
Garnish: fresh mint leaves

Combine first 3 ingredients in top of a double boiler; place over boiling water. Cook, stirring constantly, until melted.

Remove from heat, and stir in ¼ cup powdered sugar and Triple Sec. Spread mixture in pastry shell. Cool.

Place strawberries, stem side down, over chocolate mixture; brush with jelly. Chill pie 2 to 3 hours.

Beat whipping cream and 2 tablespoons powdered sugar at medium speed of an electric mixer until soft peaks form. Fold in orange rind.

Slice pie, and top each serving with a dollop of whipped cream mixture. Garnish, if desired. **Yield: one 9-inch pie.**

Fancy Fruit Tart

Sugar Cookie Pastry
Lemon Cream
½ cup fresh blueberries
½ cup fresh blackberries
½ cup grape halves
⅔ cup fresh raspberries
1 cup halved strawberries
1 peach, peeled and sliced
1 cup peach preserves

Roll Sugar Cookie Pastry into a rectangle of ⅛-inch thickness between two sheets of wax paper; chill. Remove one sheet of paper, and invert pastry into an 11- x 7½- x 1-inch tart pan, paper side up. Carefully peel away paper, and press pastry into pan.

Roll over top of tart pan with a rolling pin to trim excess pastry. (Sugar Cookie Pastry is fragile; patch with pastry trimmings, if necessary.)

Line pastry with aluminum foil, and fill foil with pastry weights or dried beans.

Bake at 375° for 15 minutes. Carefully remove foil and weights, and bake 7 additional minutes or until browned. Cool on a wire rack.

Spoon Lemon Cream into baked pastry. Arrange fruit over Lemon Cream.

Heat preserves over low heat until melted. Press preserves through a wire-mesh strainer to remove lumps. Brush strained preserves lightly over fruit. **Yield: one 11- x 7½-inch tart.**

Sugar Cookie Pastry

1¼ cups all-purpose flour
1½ tablespoons sugar
½ cup butter or margarine
3 to 4 tablespoons ice water
1 egg yolk, lightly beaten

Combine flour and sugar; cut in butter with a pastry blender until mixture is crumbly. Combine water and egg yolk; sprinkle, 1 tablespoon at a time, evenly over dry ingredients. Stir with a fork until dry ingredients are moistened.

Shape into a ball; cover and chill at least 1 hour. **Yield: pastry for one 11- x 7½-inch tart.**

Lemon Cream

4 egg yolks
⅔ cup sugar
¼ cup lemon juice
⅓ cup butter or margarine
3 tablespoons half-and-half

Combine all ingredients in a heavy saucepan, beating well. Cook mixture over medium-low heat 10 minutes or until mixture thickens, stirring constantly. Remove from heat, and cool. **Yield: 1¼ cups.**

Berry Good Lemon Tarts

½ (15-ounce) package refrigerated piecrusts
3 egg yolks
⅔ cup sugar
¼ cup lemon juice
⅓ cup butter or margarine
2 teaspoons grated lemon rind
Garnishes: blueberries, blackberries, raspberries, or strawberries

Unfold piecrust, and divide into 18 equal portions; press each portion into a 2-inch tart pan. Prick bottom of pastry generously with a fork.

Bake at 375° for 12 to 15 minutes or until lightly browned.

Combine egg yolks, sugar, and lemon juice in a small heavy saucepan, stirring until blended. Cook over low heat, stirring constantly, 5 minutes or until mixture thickens.

Remove from heat, and stir in butter and lemon rind; cool. Spoon filling evenly into tart shells. Cover and chill thoroughly. Garnish, if desired. **Yield: 1½ dozen.**

From front: Berry Good Lemon Tarts, Peachy Keen Tarts (page 119), Fancy Fruit Tart

Pecan Tart with Praline Cream

Pastry for 9-inch pie
⅓ cup butter or margarine, melted
1 cup sugar
1 cup light corn syrup
4 large eggs, beaten
1 teaspoon vanilla extract
¼ teaspoon salt
1 cup pecan halves
¼ cup semisweet chocolate morsels
½ cup whipping cream
½ teaspoon vanilla extract
1 teaspoon praline liqueur
2 tablespoons powdered sugar

Press pastry into a 9-inch tart pan with removable bottom; set aside.

Combine butter, sugar, and corn syrup in a medium saucepan; cook over low heat, stirring constantly, until sugar dissolves. Cool slightly.

Add eggs, 1 teaspoon vanilla, and salt; stir well. Pour filling into prepared pastry shell, and top with pecan halves.

Bake at 325° for 50 to 55 minutes.

Place chocolate morsels in a heavy-duty, zip-top plastic bag; seal. Submerge bag in boiling water until chocolate morsels melt. Cut a small hole in corner of bag; drizzle chocolate thinly over pecan pie.

Beat whipping cream, ½ teaspoon vanilla, and praline liqueur at medium speed of an electric mixer until foamy. Gradually add powdered sugar, beating until soft peaks form.

Spoon about 2 tablespoons whipped cream mixture onto each dessert plate. Place a slice of pie on top of cream, and serve immediately. **Yield: one 9-inch pie.**

Pecan Tart with Praline Cream

Double Pecan Pie

(pictured on page 115)

1 cup light corn syrup
¾ cup sugar
3 large eggs
3 tablespoons butter or margarine, melted
1 tablespoon brandy
1 teaspoon vanilla extract
¼ teaspoon salt
1 cup pecan pieces
Pecan Pastry
1 cup pecan halves

Combine first 7 ingredients in a medium bowl. Beat at medium speed of an electric mixer just until blended. Stir in pecan pieces.

Pour mixture into Pecan Pastry. Top with pecan halves.

Bake at 350° for 50 to 60 minutes or until set. Cover edges of pastry with aluminum foil, if necessary, to prevent excessive browning. **Yield: one 9-inch pie.**

Pecan Pastry

1 cup all-purpose flour
¼ cup ground pecans
¼ teaspoon salt
¼ cup plus 2 tablespoons butter or margarine
1 tablespoon brandy
1 to 2 tablespoons cold water

Combine first 3 ingredients in a medium bowl; cut in butter with a pastry blender until mixture is crumbly.

Sprinkle brandy over mixture, stirring with a fork. Add water, stirring just until dry ingredients are moistened. Shape pastry into a ball; cover and chill 30 minutes.

Roll pastry to ⅛-inch thickness on a lightly floured surface. Place in a 9-inch pieplate; flute edges. **Yield: pastry for one 9-inch pie.**

Peanut Butter Pie

1 (8-ounce) package cream cheese, softened
1 cup sifted powdered sugar
1 cup chunky peanut butter
½ cup milk
1 (8-ounce) container frozen whipped topping, thawed
1 (9-inch) graham cracker crust
¼ cup coarsely chopped peanuts

Combine first 4 ingredients in a large mixing bowl; beat at medium speed of an electric mixer until well blended.

Fold in whipped topping; spoon into crust, and sprinkle with peanuts. Chill 8 hours. **Yield: one 9-inch pie.**

Spirited Mince Pie

¾ cup raisins
3 tablespoons brandy
1 (15-ounce) package refrigerated piecrusts
1 teaspoon all-purpose flour
1 (27-ounce) jar mincemeat
1 large cooking apple, cored and finely chopped
1 cup chopped walnuts
¼ cup firmly packed brown sugar
1 teaspoon grated lemon or orange rind
1 tablespoon lemon juice

Combine raisins and brandy in a large bowl; let stand 2 hours.

Unfold 1 piecrust, and press out fold lines; sprinkle with flour, spreading over surface. Place, floured side down, in a 9-inch pieplate; fold edges under, and flute. Set aside.

Combine raisin mixture, mincemeat, and next 5 ingredients; spoon into pastry shell.

Roll remaining piecrust on a lightly floured surface to press out fold lines; cut with a 3¼-inch leaf-shaped cutter, and mark veins using a pastry wheel or knife. Roll pastry scraps into small balls representing berries. Arrange pastry on top of filling as desired.

Bake at 375° for 10 minutes; shield edges with aluminum foil, and bake 25 additional minutes. Cool on a wire rack. **Yield: one 9-inch pie.**

Note: You may substitute orange juice for brandy.

Harvest Pumpkin Pie

Harvest Pumpkin Pie

Pastry for double-crust 10-inch pie
3 cups cooked, mashed pumpkin
1 (12-ounce) can evaporated milk
2 large eggs, lightly beaten
1 cup sugar
¼ cup all-purpose flour
1 teaspoon vanilla extract
½ teaspoon salt
½ teaspoon ground allspice
½ teaspoon ground cinnamon
½ teaspoon ground ginger
¼ teaspoon ground cloves
¼ teaspoon ground nutmeg
1 cup whipping cream
2 tablespoons honey
2 tablespoons finely chopped pecans, toasted

Roll half of pastry to ⅛-inch thickness on a lightly floured surface. Fit into a 10-inch pieplate; trim off excess pastry along edges.

Roll remaining pastry to ⅛-inch thickness; cut leaf shapes in pastry, and mark veins using a pastry wheel or knife. Arrange leaves around edge of pieplate, reserving 6 small leaves for garnish. Set aside.

Combine pumpkin and next 11 ingredients; stir well with a wire whisk. Pour into pastry shell.

Bake at 425° for 15 minutes. Reduce heat to 350°, and bake 35 to 45 additional minutes or until a knife inserted near center comes out clean. Shield pastry leaves with strips of aluminum foil to prevent excessive browning, if necessary. Remove pie from oven, and cool completely.

Place reserved pastry leaves on an ungreased baking sheet. Bake at 450° for 6 to 8 minutes or until lightly browned. Remove to a wire rack, and cool.

Beat whipping cream at medium speed of an electric mixer until soft peaks form; fold in honey. Top pie with dollops of whipped cream; sprinkle pecans over whipped cream. Garnish with small pastry leaves. **Yield: one 10-inch pie.**

Carolina Sweet Potato Pie

1 (17-ounce) can sweet potatoes, drained and mashed
1 cup firmly packed brown sugar
⅔ cup milk
⅔ cup whipping cream
3 large eggs
3 tablespoons bourbon
1 tablespoon butter or margarine, melted
1 teaspoon ground cinnamon
½ teaspoon ground nutmeg
½ teaspoon ground ginger
¼ teaspoon salt
1 unbaked 9-inch pastry shell

Combine first 4 ingredients in a large bowl; beat at low speed of an electric mixer until smooth. Add eggs one at a time; beat after each addition. Add bourbon and next 5 ingredients; beat just until blended. Pour into pastry shell.

Bake at 375° for 50 to 55 minutes or until filling is set. Cool. **Yield: one 9-inch pie.**

Easy Lemon Chess Pie

1¾ cups sugar
2 tablespoons yellow cornmeal
¼ teaspoon salt
⅓ cup butter or margarine, melted
¼ cup evaporated milk
3 tablespoons lemon juice
4 large eggs
1 unbaked 9-inch pastry shell

Combine first 3 ingredients in a medium bowl, stirring well. Add butter, milk, and lemon juice; stir well.

Add eggs, one at a time, beating after each addition. Pour filling into pastry shell.

Bake at 350° for 45 minutes or until pie is set. Cool on a wire rack. **Yield: one 9-inch pie.**

Chocolate Dream Pie

Chocolate Dream Pie

¾ cup sugar
¼ cup cornstarch
1 tablespoon cocoa
¼ teaspoon salt
2½ cups milk
1 cup half-and-half
3 egg yolks
1 (6-ounce) package semisweet chocolate
      morsels, melted
1 teaspoon vanilla extract
Chocolate Pastry Shell
1 cup whipping cream
2 tablespoons powdered sugar
Grated semisweet chocolate

Combine first 4 ingredients in a saucepan. Add milk and half-and-half; cook over medium heat, stirring constantly, until thickened and bubbly.

Beat egg yolks at medium speed of an electric mixer until thick and pale. Gradually add one-fourth of hot mixture to yolks; add to remaining hot mixture, stirring constantly. Cook over low heat, stirring constantly, until mixture thickens. Remove from heat.

Stir in melted chocolate and vanilla. Cool completely. Pour filling into Chocolate Pastry Shell. Cover loosely; chill several hours.

Beat whipping cream at medium speed until foamy. Add powdered sugar, and beat until soft peaks form; spoon over pie. Sprinkle with grated chocolate. Garnish with pastry cutouts, if desired. **Yield: one 9-inch pie.**

Chocolate Pastry Shell
1½ cups all-purpose flour
¼ cup plus 2 tablespoons firmly packed
      brown sugar
3 tablespoons cocoa
¼ teaspoon salt
½ cup shortening
5 to 6 tablespoons cold water

Combine first 4 ingredients; cut in shortening with a pastry blender until mixture is crumbly.

Sprinkle cold water, 1 tablespoon at a time, over surface; stir with a fork until moistened. Shape into a ball; cover and chill 1 hour.

Pinch off ¼ cup pastry, and set aside to make decorative cutouts, if desired. Roll remaining pastry to ⅛-inch thickness on a floured surface. Fit into a greased 9-inch pieplate; fold edges under, and flute. Freeze 10 minutes.

Prick bottom and sides of pastry with a fork; bake at 450° for 6 to 8 minutes or until done.

Roll reserved ¼ cup pastry to ¼-inch thickness. Cut into decorative shapes, using small cookie cutters. Place on a baking sheet. Bake at 450° for 5 to 6 minutes. Cool. **Yield: enough for one 9-inch pastry shell and pastry cutouts.**

Sweetheart Fudge Pie

½ cup butter or margarine, softened
¾ cup firmly packed brown sugar
3 large eggs
1 (12-ounce) package semisweet chocolate
      morsels, melted
2 teaspoons instant coffee granules
1 teaspoon rum extract
½ cup all-purpose flour
1 cup coarsely chopped walnuts
1 unbaked 9-inch pastry shell
Garnishes: piped whipped cream, chopped
      walnuts

Beat butter at medium speed of an electric mixer until creamy; gradually add brown sugar, beating well. Add eggs, one at a time, beating after each addition.

Add melted chocolate, coffee granules, and rum extract; mix well. Stir in flour and walnuts. Spoon mixture into pastry shell.

Bake at 375° for 25 minutes; cool completely. Chill. Garnish, if desired. **Yield: 9-inch pie.**

Coffee Cream Pie

(pictured on page 2)

¼ cup butter or margarine
⅔ cup semisweet chocolate morsels
1⅓ cups graham cracker crumbs
½ cup sugar
3 tablespoons cornstarch
1 teaspoon instant coffee granules
¼ cup boiling water
1¼ cups milk
5 egg yolks, lightly beaten
1¾ cups whipping cream
¼ cup sifted powdered sugar
Garnish: chocolate-covered coffee beans

Melt butter and chocolate morsels in a heavy saucepan over low heat; stir in graham cracker crumbs. Press into a lightly greased 9-inch pieplate.

Bake at 375° for 8 minutes. Cool pie shell completely on a wire rack.

Combine ½ cup sugar and cornstarch in a large heavy saucepan; set aside.

Combine coffee granules and boiling water; stir until coffee granules dissolve. Gradually stir coffee, milk, and egg yolks into sugar mixture.

Cook over medium heat, stirring constantly, until mixture thickens and boils. Boil 1 minute, stirring constantly. Remove from heat; whisk until smooth. Place plastic wrap directly on surface of mixture; chill 1 hour.

Beat whipping cream at medium speed of an electric mixer until foamy; gradually add powdered sugar, beating until soft peaks form.

Fold 1½ cups whipped cream into coffee mixture, reserving remaining whipped cream for topping. Spoon filling into baked pie shell.

Pipe or dollop remaining cream on top of pie. Chill up to 8 hours. Garnish, if desired. **Yield: one 9-inch pie.**

Vanilla Cream Pie

¾ cup sugar
¾ cup plus 2 teaspoons cornstarch
⅛ teaspoon salt
3 egg yolks, beaten
3 cups milk
1½ tablespoons butter or margarine
1½ teaspoons vanilla extract
1 baked 9-inch pastry shell
¾ cup whipping cream
⅓ cup sifted powdered sugar

Combine first 3 ingredients in a heavy saucepan; stir well. Combine egg yolks and milk; gradually stir into sugar mixture. Cook over medium heat, stirring constantly, until mixture thickens and boils. Boil 1 minute, stirring mixture constantly.

Remove from heat; stir in butter and vanilla. Immediately pour into pastry shell. Cover filling with wax paper. Cool 30 minutes; chill until firm.

Beat whipping cream at medium speed of an electric mixer until foamy; gradually add powdered sugar, beating until soft peaks form. Spread over filling. Chill. **Yield: one 9-inch pie.**

Variations

Banana Cream Pie: Slice 2 small bananas into pastry shell before adding filling.

Butterscotch Cream Pie: Substitute ¾ cup firmly packed dark brown sugar for ¾ cup sugar; reduce vanilla to ¾ teaspoon and add ¾ teaspoon butter flavoring.

Chocolate Cream Pie: Add ¼ cup cocoa when combining sugar and cornstarch.

Coconut Cream Pie: Add ½ cup flaked coconut with vanilla. Sprinkle ¼ cup toasted flaked coconut over whipped cream.

Vanilla Cream Pie (Coconut Cream Pie variation)

Best-Ever Lemon Meringue Pie

(pictured on page 2)

1½ cups sugar
⅓ cup cornstarch
⅛ teaspoon salt
4 egg yolks
1¾ cups water
½ cup lemon juice
3 tablespoons butter or margarine
1 teaspoon grated lemon rind
1 baked 9-inch pastry shell
Meringue

Combine first 3 ingredients in a heavy saucepan; set aside.

Combine egg yolks, water, and lemon juice; stir into sugar mixture.

Cook over medium heat, stirring constantly, until mixture thickens and boils. Boil 1 minute, stirring constantly. Remove from heat.

Stir in butter and grated lemon rind. Spoon hot filling into pastry shell. Spread Meringue over hot filling, sealing to edge of pastry.

Bake at 325° for 25 to 28 minutes. **Yield: one 9-inch pie.**

Meringue

4 egg whites
½ teaspoon cream of tartar
¼ cup plus 2 tablespoons sugar
½ teaspoon vanilla extract

Beat egg whites and cream of tartar at high speed of an electric mixer until foamy. Gradually add sugar, 1 tablespoon at a time, beating until stiff peaks form and sugar dissolves (2 to 4 minutes). Beat in vanilla. **Yield: enough for one 9-inch pie.**

Lemon-Lime Meringue Pie

1⅓ cups sugar
½ cup cornstarch
⅛ teaspoon salt
1¾ cups cold water
4 large eggs, separated
3 tablespoons butter or margarine
2½ teaspoons grated lemon rind
1 teaspoon grated lime rind
2 tablespoons lime juice
2 tablespoons lemon juice
1 baked 9-inch pastry shell
½ teaspoon cream of tartar
⅓ cup sifted powdered sugar

Combine first 3 ingredients in a heavy saucepan. Gradually add water, stirring until smooth. Cook over medium heat, stirring constantly, until mixture thickens and comes to a boil. Boil 1 minute, stirring constantly. Remove from heat.

Beat egg yolks at high speed of an electric mixer until thick and pale. Gradually stir about one-fourth of hot mixture into egg yolks; add to remaining hot mixture, stirring constantly. Cook over medium heat, stirring constantly, 2 to 3 minutes.

Remove from heat. Add butter and next 4 ingredients, stirring until butter melts. Spoon hot filling into pastry shell.

Beat egg whites and cream of tartar in a large bowl at high speed 1 minute. Gradually add powdered sugar, 1 tablespoon at a time, beating until stiff peaks form and powdered sugar dissolves (2 to 4 minutes).

Spread meringue immediately over filling, sealing to edge of pastry. Bake at 325° for 25 minutes or until browned and set. Cool pie completely several hours before slicing and serving. **Yield: one 9-inch pie.**

Lemon-Lime Meringue Pie

From left: Florida Orange Pie and Key Lime Pie

Key Lime Pie

4 large eggs, separated
1 (14-ounce) can sweetened condensed milk
⅓ cup Key lime juice
½ teaspoon cream of tartar
⅓ cup sugar
1 baked 9-inch pastry shell

Combine egg yolks, condensed milk, and Key lime juice in a heavy saucepan. Cook over low heat, stirring constantly, until mixture reaches 160° (about 10 minutes).

Beat egg whites and cream of tartar at high speed of an electric mixer until foamy. Gradually add sugar, 1 tablespoon at a time, beating until stiff peaks form and sugar dissolves (2 to 4 minutes).

Pour hot filling into pastry shell. Immediately spread meringue over filling, sealing to edge.

Bake at 325° for 25 to 28 minutes. **Yield: one 9-inch pie.**

Florida Orange Pie

3 egg yolks
½ cup sugar
1 cup orange juice, divided
1 envelope unflavored gelatin
2 tablespoons grated orange rind
1 teaspoon grated lemon rind
1 pint whipping cream, divided
⅔ cup powdered sugar
⅛ teaspoon salt
½ cup flaked coconut
1 cup diced orange sections, drained
1 baked 9-inch pastry shell
3 tablespoons powdered sugar
Garnishes: toasted flaked coconut, orange sections, fresh mint

Beat egg yolks slightly. Combine yolks, ½ cup sugar, and ½ cup orange juice in a heavy saucepan.

Cook over low heat, stirring constantly, 10 to 12 minutes or until mixture reaches 160°. Remove from heat.

Sprinkle gelatin over remaining ½ cup orange juice; stir and let stand 1 minute. Add gelatin mixture and rinds to yolk mixture. Chill until consistency of unbeaten egg white.

Beat ½ cup whipping cream, ⅔ cup powdered sugar, and salt at medium speed of an electric mixer until soft peaks form.

Fold in gelatin mixture; then fold in coconut and diced orange sections. Spoon into pastry shell; chill until firm.

Beat remaining 1½ cups whipping cream until foamy; gradually add 3 tablespoons powdered sugar, beating until soft peaks form.

Spread about half of whipped cream over pie. Dollop or pipe remaining whipped cream around outer edge of pie. Garnish, if desired. **Yield: one 9-inch pie.**

Chilled Blueberry Pie

(pictured on page 117)

4 cups blueberries, divided
2 tablespoons cornstarch
2 tablespoons water
½ cup light corn syrup
2 teaspoons lemon juice
1 cup whipping cream
2 tablespoons powdered sugar (optional)
1 (9-inch) graham cracker crust
Garnishes: lemon slices, mint leaves

Puree 1 cup blueberries in an electric blender or food processor; set aside.

Combine cornstarch and water in a medium saucepan, stirring until blended. Add corn syrup, lemon juice, and blueberry puree. Bring to a boil over medium heat, stirring constantly; boil 1 minute. Cool 1 hour.

Fold remaining 3 cups blueberries into blueberry mixture. Set aside.

Beat whipping cream at medium speed of an electric mixer until foamy; gradually add powdered sugar, if desired, beating until soft peaks form. Spread in bottom and on sides of piecrust, forming a 1-inch-thick shell.

Spoon blueberry mixture into whipped cream shell. Chill at least 4 hours. Garnish, if desired. **Yield: one 9-inch pie.**

Raspberry-Sour Cream Pie

(pictured on page 2)

1 cup sugar
⅓ cup all-purpose flour
2 large eggs, lightly beaten
1⅓ cups sour cream
1 teaspoon vanilla extract
3 cups fresh raspberries
1 unbaked 9-inch pastry shell
⅓ cup all-purpose flour
⅓ cup firmly packed brown sugar
⅓ cup chopped pecans
3 tablespoons butter, softened
Garnishes: whipped cream, fresh raspberries

Combine first 5 ingredients in a large bowl, stirring until smooth. Gradually fold in raspberries. Spoon into pastry shell.

Bake at 400° for 30 to 35 minutes or until center is set.

Combine ⅓ cup flour and next 3 ingredients; sprinkle over hot pie.

Bake at 400° for 10 minutes or until golden. Cool pie before slicing and serving. Garnish, if desired. **Yield: one 9-inch pie.**

Ice Cream Pie Spectacular

1 cup graham cracker crumbs
½ cup chopped walnuts
¼ cup butter or margarine, melted
1 pint coffee ice cream, slightly softened
1 pint vanilla ice cream, slightly softened
Brown Sugar Sauce

Combine first 3 ingredients; press into a buttered 9-inch pieplate. Bake at 375° for 8 to 10 minutes; cool.

Spoon coffee ice cream evenly into cooled crust; freeze until almost firm.

Spread vanilla ice cream over coffee ice cream, and freeze until firm.

Spoon warm Brown Sugar Sauce over slices. **Yield: one 9-inch pie.**

Brown Sugar Sauce

3 tablespoons butter or margarine
1 cup firmly packed brown sugar
½ cup half-and-half
1 cup chopped walnuts
1 teaspoon vanilla extract

Melt butter in a heavy saucepan over low heat; add brown sugar. Cook 5 to 6 minutes, stirring constantly.

Remove from heat, and gradually stir in half-and-half. Return to heat, and cook 1 minute.

Remove from heat, and stir in walnuts and vanilla. **Yield: about 1½ cups.**

Peppermint Ice Cream Pie

2 (1-ounce) squares semisweet chocolate
½ cup butter or margarine
2 large eggs
1 cup sugar
½ cup all-purpose flour
⅛ teaspoon salt
1 quart peppermint ice cream, slightly softened
½ cup hot fudge sauce
2 cups whipping cream
½ cup finely crushed peppermint candy
Peppermint candy pieces

Combine chocolate and butter in a small saucepan; cook over medium-low heat, stirring occasionally, until chocolate and butter melt. Remove from heat; cool.

Beat eggs at medium speed of an electric mixer until thick and pale; gradually add sugar, beating well.

Combine flour and salt, stirring well.

Add flour and chocolate mixtures to egg mixture, beating just until blended. Heavily grease and flour the bottom of a 10-inch pieplate. Spread batter evenly in prepared pieplate.

Bake at 350° for 30 to 40 minutes or until done. Cool completely.

Spoon ice cream over cooled crust; freeze 1 hour. Drizzle fudge sauce over ice cream; swirl fudge gently into ice cream with a knife. Freeze several hours or until firm.

Beat whipping cream at medium speed until soft peaks form. Gently fold in crushed peppermint candy. Pipe or spoon whipped cream in a decorative design over top of frozen pie. Freeze 30 minutes.

Decorate top of pie with peppermint candy pieces. Let pie stand at room temperature 5 to 10 minutes before slicing and serving. **Yield: one 10-inch pie.**

Peppermint Ice Cream Pie

Grasshopper Pie

Grasshopper Pie

1¼ cups chocolate wafer crumbs (about 32 wafers)
⅓ cup butter or margarine, melted
1 (6-ounce) package chocolate-covered mint wafer candies
4 cups miniature marshmallows
¼ cup sugar
2 tablespoons butter or margarine
⅓ cup green crème de menthe
1½ cups whipping cream, whipped

Combine chocolate crumbs and melted butter; press evenly over bottom and sides of a greased 9-inch pieplate.

Bake at 350° for 6 to 8 minutes. Cool crust completely.

Cut 3 mint candies diagonally in half; set aside. Reserve 10 whole candies for garnish. Chop remaining candies; set aside.

Combine marshmallows, sugar, and 2 tablespoons butter in top of a double boiler. Bring water to a boil. Reduce heat to low; cook until marshmallows melt, stirring frequently.

Remove from heat. Stir in crème de menthe. Cool mixture to room temperature. Fold in chopped mint candies and whipped cream.

Spread mixture evenly into prepared crust. Arrange reserved candy halves in a circle in center of pie; freeze until firm.

Pull a vegetable peeler down sides of reserved whole candies to make tiny shavings. Garnish pie with candy shavings. **Yield: one 9-inch pie.**

Frozen Chocolate Pie with Pecan Crust

6 (1-ounce) squares semisweet chocolate
½ teaspoon instant coffee granules
2 large eggs, beaten
3 tablespoons Kahlúa
¼ cup powdered sugar
¾ cup whipping cream
1 teaspoon vanilla extract
Pecan Crust
¾ cup whipping cream
1 tablespoon Kahlúa
Grated chocolate

Combine chocolate squares and coffee granules in a saucepan over low heat; cook, stirring constantly, until melted. Stir one-fourth of melted chocolate into eggs; mix well. Add to remaining chocolate. Stir in 3 tablespoons Kahlúa and sugar.

Cook, stirring constantly, until mixture reaches 160°. Cool to room temperature.

Beat ¾ cup whipping cream at medium speed of an electric mixer until soft peaks form; fold into chocolate mixture. Stir in vanilla.

Spoon into cooled Pecan Crust. Cover; freeze. Transfer pie to refrigerator 1 hour before serving.

Beat ¾ cup whipping cream at medium speed until foamy; gradually add 1 tablespoon Kahlúa, beating until soft peaks form. Pipe or dollop whipped cream around edge of pie. Sprinkle with grated chocolate. **Yield: one 9-inch pie.**

Pecan Crust
2 cups coarsely chopped pecans
⅓ cup firmly packed brown sugar
3 tablespoons butter or margarine, melted
2 teaspoons Kahlúa

Combine all ingredients; press evenly over bottom and up sides of a 9-inch pieplate.

Bake at 350° for 10 to 12 minutes. Press sides with back of spoon. Cool. **Yield: one 9-inch crust.**

Apple Cobbler à la Mode

Apple Cobbler à la Mode

6 cups peeled, sliced cooking apples
1 cup chopped walnuts
½ cup firmly packed brown sugar
1 teaspoon ground cinnamon
1 cup all-purpose flour
1 teaspoon baking powder
¼ teaspoon salt
1 cup sugar
¼ teaspoon ground ginger
1 large egg, beaten
½ cup half-and-half
½ cup butter or margarine, melted
½ cup chopped walnuts
Vanilla ice cream

Combine first 4 ingredients; toss gently. Spread in a greased 11- x 7- x 1½-inch baking dish.

Combine flour and next 4 ingredients in a bowl; stir well. Combine egg, half-and-half, and butter. Add to flour mixture; stir just until blended. Pour over apple mixture; sprinkle with ½ cup walnuts.

Bake at 350° for 45 minutes to 1 hour or until lightly browned. Spoon warm cobbler into serving bowls, and top with ice cream. **Yield: 8 servings.**

Juicy Blackberry Cobbler

(pictured on page 117)

4 cups fresh blackberries or 2 (16-ounce)
   packages frozen blackberries, thawed
1 cup sugar
½ cup water
Pastry
2 tablespoons butter, melted and divided
2 tablespoons sugar, divided

Combine first 3 ingredients in a saucepan. Cook over medium heat 10 minutes; stir gently.

Pour half of berry mixture into a greased 12- x 8- x 2-inch baking dish.

Roll pastry to ⅛-inch thickness on a floured surface. Cut into 1-inch strips; arrange half of strips in a lattice design over berry mixture. Brush with 1 tablespoon melted butter; sprinkle with 1 tablespoon sugar. Bake at 375° for 10 to 12 minutes or until pastry is lightly browned.

Pour remaining berry mixture over baked pastry. Arrange remaining strips in lattice design over berries. Brush with remaining butter; sprinkle with remaining sugar. Bake at 375° for 20 minutes or until pastry is golden. **Yield: 6 servings.**

Pastry

1½ cups all-purpose flour
¾ teaspoon salt
½ cup shortening
5 tablespoons cold water

Combine flour and salt; cut in shortening with a pastry blender until mixture is crumbly.

Sprinkle water, 1 tablespoon at a time, evenly over surface; stir with a fork until dry ingredients are moistened. Shape into a ball; cover and chill. **Yield: pastry for 1 cobbler.**

Strawberry-Rhubarb Cobbler

2 cups cubed rhubarb (about 1 pound)
2 cups halved strawberries
1 cup sugar
1½ tablespoons quick-cooking tapioca
⅛ teaspoon salt
2 tablespoons butter or margarine
Pastry for 8-inch pie

Combine first 5 ingredients; toss. Spoon into a greased 8-inch square baking dish. Dot with butter.

Roll pastry to ⅛-inch thickness on a lightly floured surface; cut into ½-inch strips, and arrange in a lattice design over rhubarb mixture.

Bake at 375° for 40 to 45 minutes or until pastry is golden. **Yield: 6 servings.**

Crusty Peach Cobbler

Crusty Peach Cobbler

7 to 7½ cups sliced fresh peaches
1½ to 2 cups sugar
2 to 4 tablespoons all-purpose flour
½ teaspoon ground nutmeg
1 teaspoon almond or vanilla extract
⅓ cup butter or margarine
Pastry for double-crust pie
Vanilla ice cream

Combine first 4 ingredients in a Dutch oven; set aside until syrup forms.

Bring peach mixture to a boil; reduce heat to low, and cook 10 minutes or until peaches are tender. Remove from heat; stir in almond extract and butter.

Roll half of pastry to ⅛-inch thickness on a lightly floured surface; cut into a 9-inch square. Spoon half of peach mixture into a lightly buttered 9-inch square dish; top with pastry square.

Bake at 425° for 14 minutes or until lightly browned. Spoon remaining peach mixture over baked pastry square.

Roll remaining pastry to ⅛-inch thickness, and cut into 1-inch strips; arrange in lattice design over peach mixture.

Bake at 425° for 15 to 18 minutes or until browned. Spoon into serving bowls, and top with ice cream. **Yield: 8 servings.**

Peach Cobbler with Praline Biscuits

1½ cups sugar
2 tablespoons cornstarch
1 teaspoon ground cinnamon
1 cup water
8 cups sliced fresh peaches (about 5½ pounds)
3 tablespoons butter or margarine, melted
¼ cup firmly packed dark brown sugar
1 cup chopped pecans
2 cups self-rising flour
2 teaspoons sugar
½ cup shortening
¾ cup buttermilk

Combine first 3 ingredients in a Dutch oven. Gradually stir in water; add peaches. Bring to a boil, and cook 1 minute, stirring often.

Remove from heat. Pour into a lightly greased 13- x 9- x 2-inch baking dish; set aside.

Combine butter, brown sugar, and pecans; set mixture aside.

Combine flour and 2 teaspoons sugar; cut in shortening with a pastry blender until mixture is crumbly. Add buttermilk, stirring just until dry ingredients are moistened. Turn dough out onto a floured surface, and knead 3 or 4 times.

Roll dough to a 12- x 8-inch rectangle; spread with reserved pecan mixture, leaving a ½-inch border. Starting with long side, roll up jellyroll fashion. Cut into ½-inch slices; arrange slices over peach mixture.

Bake at 400° for 25 to 30 minutes or until lightly browned. **Yield: 12 servings.**

Index